André Malraux

AN AGE OF OPPRESSION

(Le Temps du mépris)

Cover illustration:
"For the prisoners…time was like a giant black spider…swinging to and fro…" (*An Age of Oppression*, p.18).

This edition published in Paperback in UK in 2003 by
Elm Bank, an imprint of Intellect Ltd, PO Box 862, Bristol BS99 1DE, UK

This edition published in Paperback in USA in 2003 by
Elm Bank, ISBS, 5824 N.E. Hassalo St, Portland, Oregon 97213-3644, USA

Consulting Editor: Keith Cameron
Cover Illustration: R. A. E. Newnham
Cover Design: Peter Singh

A catalogue record for this book is available from the British Library

ISBN 1-84150-854-3

Printed and bound in Great Britain by Antony Rowe Ltd, Eastbourne.

André Malraux

AN AGE OF
OPPRESSION

(Le Temps du mépris)

Translated by Roberta A. E. Newnham

Elm Bank

Bristol, UK
Portland, OR, USA

Acknowledgements

I wish to thank André Malraux's publishers, Gallimard, of Paris, for granting me permission to publish this translation. I should also like to express my grateful thanks to Professor Keith Cameron for his kind interest and assistance at various stages during the research and compilation of this annotated text. Thanks also to Trevor Learmouth of the University of Exeter Library and to Angela Foster for her typing assistance.
Finally, I owe a special debt of gratitude to my family Kirsten, Leah and Sam for their unfailing moral support and encouragement.

CONTENTS

Introduction vii

Translator's Note xiii

An Age of Oppression

Author's Preface 1

Chapter I 4

Chapter II 14

Chapter III 22

Chapter IV 28

Chapter V 34

Chapter VI 42

Chapter VII 49

Chapter VIII 56

Notes to the Text 63

Biographical Summary 68

Select Bibliography 72

INTRODUCTION

For many years after it was first published in 1935, following its initial serialisation in the N.R.F. literary periodical,[1] André Malraux's *Le Temps du mépris* was out of print and virtually unobtainable in the U.K. It has, however, been included in the new *Pléiade* edition of the author's complete works which Gallimard is publishing to commemorate his centenary in 2001.

Unlike its widely acclaimed predecessor, *La Condition humaine*,[2] which won Malraux the *Prix Goncourt* following its publication in 1933, his short story, *Le Temps du mépris*, a *nouvelle* set in early 1930s Germany, was received with considerably less enthusiasm by the critics of the time. Regarded somewhat dismissively as being more political propaganda rather than a work of fiction, it has since remained largely sidelined compared with the majority of his other literary works until its recent republication in 1997.[3]

A highly evocative and menacingly claustrophobic atmosphere, which characterised much of the action in *La Condition humaine*, together with the portrayal of the psychological state of the main protagonists as they met in secret, frequently under cover of darkness, to organise their doomed campaign, are similarly focal features of *Le Temps du mépris*, but this time the action is set in a European context. The chief protagonist, Kassner, a German national — normally resident in Prague — who is also a committed anti-Fascist and a wanted Communist activist working undercover in Germany, is arrested by Nazi soldiers. He is interrogated, but not recognised by his captors as a wanted person, and is put into solitary confinement in what he soon realises is no ordinary prison but, in fact, a concentration camp. Alone in his cell, cut off from the world and normality, he suffers a mental breakdown but is eventually released after a fellow Communist, passing himself off as the "real" Kassner, gives himself up, probably at the sacrifice of his own life. After his release, Kassner survives a hurricane during his clandestine plane journey back to Prague, where he searches in vain for his wife at a Party rally but is eventually reunited with her and their child.

Much of the action of *Le Temps du mépris* focuses upon Kassner's psychological deterioration and increasingly manic behaviour as he endures day after day of isolation and sensory deprivation in his pitch-dark cell, under the constant threat of torture and exposed to the screams of other suffering prisoners. He begins to drift in

---

[1] *La Nouvelle Revue Française*, 23e année, 1935, mars, n° 258: 396-427; avril, n° 259: 546-574; mai, n° 260: 728-745.

[2] Malraux's celebrated novel inspired by the struggles of the Communist revolutionaries in China, particularly Shanghai, during the 1920s.

[3] The edition used for the purposes of this translation was the 1935 (1st) edition of the text published by Gallimard, which contains an amended and more complete version of the original three articles in the form of a short story. The 1935 edition also carries a prefixing dedication, by Malraux to his German comrades, which has not been included in the 1997 republished version.

and out of conscious awareness of reality and experiences a series of "flashbacks" and hallucinatory visions (triggered by a familiar tune hummed by a passing guard), which, in his more lucid moments, he attempts to organise into a cognitive defence mechanism: not only to preserve his sanity but also to avoid betraying vital Party secrets. He is finally saved from utter, irreversible breakdown by a fellow-prisoner in an adjacent cell who establishes a form of communication with him by tapping out messages of support on their communal wall. For a long while after his release, Kassner remains traumatised by his experiences in the prison-camp. Obsessive thoughts continually haunt him and he finds normal inter-personal communication virtually impossible, remaining distant and preoccupied even when he reaches the safety of his own home in Prague.

As post-World War II history has shown, when the Nazi concentration camps were opened up by the Allies in 1945 and the horrific scale of the barbaric torture and death suffered by those considered "undesirables" by the Nazis — while survivors of the camps told of the physical and psychological trauma they had endured — Europeans, mindful of the not so distant horrors of the first World War, were at a loss to understand how such unspeakable evil had been allowed to fester, almost unheeded, and wreak such terrible human devastation in their midst.

Yet, in 1935, here in *Le Temps du mépris,* Malraux was already sounding a public warning — outside Germany — dedicating his *nouvelle* to his German anti-Fascist comrades and their heroic spirit and endurance. Whether or not the story was perceived as mere propaganda — it later became known that the author himself did not rate it highly among his literary works, calling it a "un navet"[4] (a flop) — several themes already present in his earlier novels feature prominently in the evolution of the action. In *Le Temps du mépris,* the depiction of disturbing crises of identity, obsessions, alienation and lack of communication is counter-balanced by that of more positive forms of will-power and "virile fraternity" — masculine solidarity inspiring courage and hope in the face of physical adversity or ideological oppression. Like the evocation of the prison's morbid, menacing atmosphere and the massed, black storm clouds of the hurricane — metaphors surely for the threat of Facist totalitarianism which loomed over Europe during the 1930s — these themes assume a disquieting topical relevance in the context of contemporary events, the dramatic prelude to the second World War.[5] It was this latter aspect of the work, together with its political and humanitarian undertones, which inspired Albert Camus to adapt Malraux's *nouvelle* for the theatre and to stage it as the opening production of his Théâtre du Travail in Algiers in 1936.[6]

---

[4] Cf. R.Stéphane. *Fin d'une jeunesse,* Paris, 1954, p. 51.

[5] Malraux would later return to a similar but more complex thematic base in *L'Espoir* (1937) in which the action centres upon the International Brigade's participation in the Spanish Civil War, and again in *Les Noyers de l'Altenburg* (1943) which focuses upon the wartime experiences of an Alsatian father, fighting on the German side in World War I, but narrated by his son, a French World War II prisoner of war.

[6] Cf. Olivier Todd, *Camus,* Paris: Gallimard, 1996, p. 122.

Like several other French intellectuals of the inter-War period, Malraux was very much politically aware, acquiring a reputation for his left-wing views and literary activism. Having travelled extensively during the 1920s, notably in Indo-China as an archaeological explorer and later in China and Russia as an active fellow-traveller of the Communists (although never a fully paid-up member of the Party), he resurfaced in 1930s Europe, between his travels, as a committed "man of action". For him, along with other men of ideas, such as Gide and Camus, writing and journalism became political weapons to combat the rising tide of Fascism in Europe.

In Malraux's case, his political activities also involved campaigning against anti-Semitism, for human rights and freedom from all totalitarian oppression. After the Reichstag Fire in 1933,[7] when instant reprisals were taken in Germany against leading intellectuals and many prominent Communists were imprisoned[8] he campaigned publicly on their behalf. Between the years 1933-34 he played an active role in organising the defence of several key Communist activists, notably Ernst Thälmann and Georgi Dimitrov, and travelled to Germany with André Gide to attend the trials, which in Dimitrov's case was to end successfully by his acquittal in December 1933.

Thälmann was to remain in prison for several years and a renewed appeal for his release was launched at the opening performance of Camus' production of *Le Temps du mépris* in Algiers. It is worth noting, in view of its relevance to the original *nouvelle,* that the German Communist Thälmann was widely believed to have been the author's model for Kassner, although the latter was portrayed as a democrat in Camus' play.[9]

Such then was the background to this concise but compelling story which provides a unique insight into the potentially traumatic consequences of rampant Fascism, particularly Nazism, which threatened an apparently heedless Europe during this critical pre-war period.

Apart from its historical and sociological relevance, *Le Temps du mépris* also marks a significant moment in the evolution of Malraux's fictional *oeuvre*. In this *nouvelle,* which has been likened to a Promethean prose-poem by a more sympathetic critic,[10] Malraux's previous tendencies to touch upon the psychological motivation of men of action are refined and the focus is upon the effects that solitary confinement, and sensory deprivation, plus the threat of torture and ultimate death, have upon the inner world of the spirit: the motivation, will-power and emotions of a victim of Nazi repression — in this case, a political prisoner. Malraux's next novel, *L'Espoir*, with its more journalistic, episodic narrative style, would concentrate rather upon the "outer"

---

[7] Significantly, also the year the Dachau and Oranienburg concentration camps were established and the anti-Jewish campaign began in earnest. Communists, trade-unionists and other "undesirables" were also targeted.

[8] This despite the fact that not long afterwards, the arsonists were discovered to be disaffected members of Hitler's own party, the NSDAP, later the National Socialist Party.

[9] Todd, op.cit., p. 123.

[10] Cf. C. Jenkins, *André Malraux*, New York: Twayne Publishers Inc., 1972, pp. 83-4.

world of the politics, action and events of the Spanish Civil War, the moral and ethical dilemmas it posed and a more wide-ranging and relaxed form of inter-personal communication between the leading protagonists.

It could be argued that, reduced to its basic *leitmotiv, Le Temps du mépris* is the portrayal of a battle between the will to survive (Kassner/Communist altruism) and the will to power (Nazism/totalitarian oppression). The *nouvelle's* title was believed by Camus, among others, to have been inspired by Friedrich Nietzsche's *Thus Spoke Zarathustra.*[11] The German philosopher had developed his theory that man had lost his sense of identity, dignity and traditional belief in the meaning of existence (hence his purpose and rightful place in the order of things) through a psychologically misguided adherence to religious and/or moral beliefs. Nietzsche held that man should cultivate his will-power and use this, as an absolute value in itself, in his quest for self-perfection and thus the justification for his existence. Viewed from this perspective and in the light of Malraux's lifelong interest in Nietzsche's philosophy and writings (already apparent when he embarked upon his Indo-China adventures as a young man), the tragic irony and symbolism inherent in the author's choice of such a title for his *nouvelle,* with its interrelated philosophical and historical connotations, would appear to be eminently justified.

First and foremost, *Le Temps du mépris* is the tale of a psychological drama induced by a quasi-Kafkaesque situation in which a Nazi attempt at alienating a prisoner from his inner self, through the powerful weapons of repressive confinement and physical or mental brutality, is tellingly portrayed. This attempt to reduce an "undesirable" human-being to a primeval non-being is juxtaposed with the example of the fight and ultimate survival of the inner self against the odds, through the solidarity and kindred spirit the victim musters autonomously or experiences, in body or in mind, with his fellow comrades. It is not surprising that, in his *Préface* to the book, Malraux alluded to the world and action depicted in his *nouvelle* as pertaining to the world of Classical tragedy.

From the rather torpid quality of the opening scene, in which the hero as victim, the trained militant, slowly takes in the situation, his gaze shifting from one to the other of the two people engaged in the power-game taking place in the guard-room, then contemplates his own imminent interrogation, his mind flickering back to the altruistic reason for his own arrest, the lack of physical momentum heightens the latent atmosphere of impending doom. From this ominous, quasi-cinematic prelude to the main drama, we witness Kassner's inexorable downward spiral into the nether regions of his mind, climaxing with the Dantesque visions and nightmarish dream-sequence when he temporarily loses control.

Symbols and images reminiscent of Zarathustra's universe (and also of Malraux's earlier novels) pepper the narrative from the constant allusions to the gloomy darkness of Kassner's cell to the dark despair of his fraught mind. He, too, becomes obsessed by insects: by swinging spiders, pendulum-like symbols of the passing of time; and by recurring images of the prison's population as millipedes, termites and ants which become metaphors for the insignificance of man in a vast, indifferent

---

[11] Cf. G. Brée, *Camus,* New Jersey: Rutgers University Press, 1959, p. 33n.

universe, as he visualises them busily scurrying around in an endless, seemingly meaningless mission to nowhere.

This phantasmagorical aspect inevitably heightens the *nouvelle*'s psychological overtones. At first, involuntarily transported into a fantasy-world by the association of ideas prompted by the musical stimulus he hears, fearful and lonely in his enforced solitude, Kassner becomes involved in a desperate tussle between his consciousness and sub-consciousness. The obsessive image of a vulture pecking at his flesh seems to become virtually synonymous with the manner in which the music tears at his heart-strings or with the guards' jackboots mercilessly kicking him. Kassner manifests a whole range of psychological disorders and irrational phobias, not least his obsessive-compulsive trotting around his cell and counting: needing to get to one hundred by a certain time otherwise his wife would die. At other times he intentionally escapes from nightmarish reality into the comforting world of illusions. Later, he becomes pathologically obsessed with his nails and his hand — for him a potential instrument for committing suicide — the hand being a well-known metaphor in escapist or nightmare fantasies. In these it can be seen as an instrument of torture or even an agent of doom. It is also said to symbolise lack of responsibility for a person's actions, taking on a disembodied quality and "acting" independently, thereby absolving its owner from liability or moral blame.

Again, from time to time, Kassner understandably exhibits symptoms of the "fight or flight" response or survival mechanism: either when, temples throbbing and heart racing, he is totally caught up in one of his action-packed, fast moving fantasies or panicking in adrenaline-filled apprehension of actual physical danger.

Summoned back to reality on more than one occasion by his neighbouring prisoner's faithful attempts at communication, or by the realisation that some intrusive noise effect in one of his visions is the actual scream of a fellow-prisoner being tortured, Kassner's two worlds continue to collide until his release. Later, feelings of unreality or alienation continue to obsess him. In fact, he increasingly demonstrates signs of what is now termed "post-traumatic stress disorder"; he continues to be haunted by his memories, throughout the horrendous experience of his escape through the hurricane, the cathartic walk through the streets of Prague and his participation in the Party rally, until the final *dénouement*: the reunion with his family and ultimate convincing return to the real world.

The structure of the plot of *Le Temps du mépris* itself poses an intriguing conundrum. Kassner, during his many escapist fantasies and dreams, frequently loses himself in revolutionary folklore and legendary Communist exploits, rather than his own personal experiences. From a chronological standpoint, he had to be too young to have witnessed at first hand many of the horrific scenes he "relives" and which terrorise his subconscious. Again, whether or not the hurricane episode, based on Malraux's own adventurous flight over the Yemen desert with a friend early in 1934, and mentioned again in his "memoirs",[12] was merely tacked on (as some critics believed) as padding to a rather bare plot in order to provide a catharsis to the main drama, it could be argued that the episode enhances both the physical and

---

[12] *Antimémoires*, Gallimard, Paris, 1967.

psychological elements of the action. It is, after all, perfectly feasible, given such a chain of events, that a political refugee from Germany, fleeing over the mountains in a light plane in perilous weather conditions, could undergo such an experience.

Despite the adverse reaction to his *nouvelle,* we can say that Malraux succeeded in graphically portraying what was, in retrospect, a prophetic vision of the potential repercussions for the psyche of a victim of the Nazi, or indeed of any, inhumane totalitarian regime. Sadly, this is a situation only too familiar to today's readers acquainted with e.g. the histories of Vietnam, Cambodia, Latin-America and the internecine conflagrations in what was formerly the Republic of Yugoslavia. At the same time, despite the propagandist aspect of *Le Temps du mépris,* he was not only highlighting a moment in European history which prompted Camus to declare that "Notre XXe siècle est le siècle de la peur"[13] but, as in the manner of Classical tragedy, he was also illustrating an eternal truth. Evil incarnate may lay waste in the physical sense but will never destroy what binds together all men of goodwill who carry on the timeless fight against injustice and oppression: the continuity of the spirit and will to survive that are an eternal part of man's essential being. The work of contemporary humanitarian organisations bears witness to that inviolable truth. For what else was so much of the 20th century, for so many people, nations even, if not an age of oppression?

Le Temps du mépris makes for an absorbing read on more than one level. This translation will interest those who wish to familiarise themselves with the lesser-known works of André Malraux, or to expand their knowledge of pre-World War II French fiction. For the non-francophone or non-linguistically orientated reader in general, it offers an insight into pre-War European history and social-psychology, particularly regarding the ramifications of rampant Nazism within Germany and the price paid by defenders of human rights. It should, perhaps, not be forgotten that this is the story of what happened to a politically incorrect German national, an "undesirable", yet portrayed through the eyes of a Frenchman!

---

[13] Cf. *Albert Camus: Selected Political Writing*, ed. J. H. King, London: Methuen Educational Ltd, 1981, 'Ni Victimes ni Bourreaux', p. 79.

TRANSLATOR'S NOTE

For the translator, the main aim must be to produce a readable rendition of a foreign-language text, whilst remaining faithful to the spirit which inspired the original. Furthermore, in the particular case of *Le Temps du mépris*, the primary concern is to make what, to some, may be a work of propaganda, yet nevertheless deserves a sympathetic reading, both interesting and appealing to the English reader. The translated version has not only to "go with the flow" of its original guiding inspiration but also to literally flow in its English version so as to absorb and maintain the interest of its reader.

This criterion, however, when applied to a work such as *Le Temps du mépris* can immediately give rise to a potential problem, particularly with regard to the author's style and the linguistic "flavour" of the rather stilted forms of expression of the 1930s. Many of the literary purists' main criticisms have been levelled at Malraux's characteristically elliptical, somewhat esoteric narrative technique, with its occasionally inconsistent syntax or tense sequence and cryptic (often chaotic) imagery and allusions. Nevertheless, such aspects of his technique which have been considered as a stylist "handicap" could be regarded as peculiarly apposite devices, consistent with the nature of its subject-matter, in this particular *nouvelle*. Here, the terse, idiosyncratic syntax is reminiscent to Anglo-Saxons and others, of the somewhat stilted Germanic form of dialectic, while the abundance of visual or synaesthetic images are uniquely suited to the evocative description of Kassner's tension-fraught experiences as a militant, his curt exchanges with the Nazis and the portrayal of his mental turmoil and encroaching madness as he lurches between reality and illusion, brooding alone in his cell. This is equally true of the atmosphere of latent violence which pervades the action throughout — from his arrest to the eventual uneasy serenity of his homecoming. Thus, syntax and punctuation have, in the main, followed those of the original text. This is especially noticeable in Chapter II where, at repeated intervals, Kassner is trying to tap out answering messages to his neighbour, racking his brains for some sort of code to use, constantly on the alert for the sound of an approaching guard, fearing their tapping might be overheard. In such instances the jerky, elliptical syntax of the original has been maintained: so the terse "Silence" or "Nothing" — directly translating — "Rien" — have been left, rather than a more elegant type of sentence e.g. "not a sound could be heard" substituted. The simple words are more effective by far, vividly conveying Kassner's suspense as he feverishly knocks then listens, quickly registers the fact that no one is either replying or listening outside his cell and nervously carries on.

This is a typical moment in the narrative which constantly alternates between the subjective *monologue intérieur* (stream of consciousness) as we see the action through Kassner's eyes or thoughts, and the more objective third-person perspective through which we observe the various events and the consequent effect they have on him — whether he is dreaming, racing round his cell, heroically battling against the hurricane or safe at home.

Where over-adherence to the original elliptical syntax or punctuation might confuse, e.g. where it may be unclear whether Kassner is thinking or voicing his thoughts aloud while rambling — both physically and mentally — around his cell, terrified that his wife may be dead, vocabulary and punctuation have been modified at times and a phrase such as "… he mumbled aloud" inserted, to give the narrative flow greater clarity and coherence.

In the "dream sequence" (Chapters II and III), in which Kassner drifts between nightmarish vision and complete mental alienation from his inner self, but is then pulled back from the brink by some noise or other, forcing him back into real time and lucidity, the frequently over-long, image-laden sentences of the French original, which may appear too convoluted and possibly confusing, to an Anglo-Saxon reader have also been paraphrased and/or repunctuated. In this specific section full stops, colons or semi-colons have either been inserted or repositioned and new paragraphs created. Again, where deemed to be contextually appropriate, subjective or impersonal tense forms have been elided and shorter structures such as "he'd", "who've" and "there's" have been used both here and elsewhere in the text. Rather than inhibiting narrative continuity, these somewhat radical modifications will, hopefully, enhance the original text's graphic portrayal of the hero's progressive mental instability and cognitive withdrawal from reality. Similar, but less radical, modifications have been made elsewhere in the text, e.g. in the later chapters, so as to conserve the momentum of the rapidly evolving mental and physical action.

In this "dream sequence", difficulties arise with the author's frequently inconsistent use of various tenses: notably the alternation between Past and Present. These have been modified at times and one particular form of the relevant tense substituted where appropriate, e.g. in the descriptions of the attack on the religious procession or elsewhere in flashbacks to revolutionary incidents, in order to provide greater coherence unless the inconsistency of tense use clearly contributes to the graphic representation of Kassner's rambling state of mind. In such instances, the Present tense accentuates the fact that he is reliving a past event in all its vivid detail and into which we are drawn by the more "immediate" nature of this particular tense, thus its use has been retained in this translation.

A similar decision had to be taken concerning semantics and phraseology. Kassner refers variously to his prison-cell as "cellule" (prison-cell) or "cachot" (cell/dungeon) — the latter, more medieval term aptly conveying his trauma at being confined in the hostile, dark bowels of the prison-camp, constantly dreading the consequences of some form of sadistic, medieval-like torture. According to Kassner's apparent frame of mind at the time: whether he is brooding obsessively, simply thinking or later talking in the abstract about his experiences, the more contextually appropriate term has been used.

Kassner's verbal "tic" or habitual expression — "voyez-vous bien" — equally poses a challenge. It is used variously throughout, mostly in totally dissimilar contexts. However, what may be used with an identical syntactic structure but with a different semantic emphasis in a variety of circumstances in French would not always have the appropriate semantic resonance when similarly employed in English. Therefore, depending upon whether Kassner is using the expression when talking to the Nazis or elsewhere as a form of conversational emphasis in a more informal context, the translated version has accordingly been modified or paraphrased to: "as you may see for yourselves" or "as you may imagine" for the more subservient phrases used to address the Nazis or to "…d'you see" or "… you can imagine", a more rhetorical form, or even "would you believe", when he is talking in less formal circumstances.

Visual images or substantive epithets such as "Escargot" can also pose dilemmas for a translator. Used in the original French text to describe the stylistic *mélange* of the wealthy Tsarists' baroque furniture, translated as: "… a combination of Louis XV and 'Escargot'…," no such term would appear to exist, either in annals of furnishing terminology or in antique-collectors' jargon. It therefore has to be a neologism (and possibly the sole attempt at humour in the whole *nouvelle!), a disparaging visual image concocted by Malraux himself to depict the convoluted, twisted forms typical of the over-ornate Baroque style in art, architecture or, in this case, furniture — a style unbeloved of many discerning "amateurs", it would appear. At the same time, of course, it graphically conveys the revolutionary's contempt for the wealthy classes and bourgeois values in general. While the term "Escargot" has been retained in the translated text, the literal English equivalent ("snail"), which retains the visually evocative but, to some, equally repellent connotation has been adhered to in the Notes section.

The temptation to over-translate or interpret can also occur when the translator is faced with a "loaded" image such as that of the vulture in the dream sequence. Since the heraldic emblem depicted on the German national flag is that of an eagle (symbolic of the state's historical associations with the Roman Empire), it is tempting to use that uniquely evocative national symbol at some stage. Nevertheless, such fanciful self-indulgence must be dismissed: Malraux used the term "vautour" and so "vulture" it must be, particularly since the image of that voracious bird of prey — with its sadistic appetite for gorging itself on dead carcasses — graphically evokes not only the possibly subconscious metaphorical allusion to the national heraldic symbol but also to the Nazi regime's sadistic repression and torture of thousands of "undesirables". The vision of a vulture literally preys on Kassner's mind over and over again as, for example, he imagines being shut in a cage with the monstrous bird tearing at his flesh during one of his nightmares or visualises its silhouette formed on the ground by lifeless corpses lying strewn about after a battle.

A more basic linguistic challenge presents itself concerning culturally-specific references where French terminology is used. The text is littered with a profusion of historical and quasi-factual allusions, most frequently relating to the history of Communist or other revolutionary action — including riots, massacres and wars — and spanning at least one generation. The problem was to make these contextually identifiable for the English reader without prejudicing narrative continuity. The best, if somewhat imperfect, solution appeared to be to substitute the original's French versions of specific Proper Nouns and historical allusions with anglicised or internationally-recognisable versions in the translated text, adding footnote reference – marks on the relevant page and providing further elucidation in the Notes to the Text appendix. It is hoped that, in this way, the reader may enjoy an uninterrupted reading of the translation whilst having the benefit of a brief reference section to hand and without needing recourse to the nearest library!

Since the story is set in Germany, the place-name "Polizei-Präsidium" has been spelt in the vernacular with its English equivalent (Police H.Q.) inserted immediately afterwards. The less familiar acronym, the SA (as opposed to the infamous SS) has been explained briefly in the Notes to the Text, along with other more cryptic allusions such as those to the Orthodox religious processions, wending their way across the plain to be attacked en route, that haunt Kassner during his terror-stricken reveries.

Despite all such paradoxes and whatever the limitations imposed by an author's linguistic idiosyncrasies, the ultimate goal for the translator remains that of conveying the meaning of the target foreign-language text. The choice of nuanced idiom will be dictated by its tone, mood and message and, it is hoped, will thus provide a fluent and rewarding version of the original text for the reader.

AUTHOR'S PREFACE

Following its publication in a review, the opinions expressed by some critics in their articles concerning this short story have prompted me to take this opportunity of briefly outlining a few of the ideas which I intend to develop elsewhere.

I would refer those who consider my factual references as being somewhat sketchy to the *official* regulations regarding concentration camps. I am not implying that prison-camps are a defining characteristic of the German National Socialist Party alone; the little we know about our own French labour camps is hardly encouraging; but it is most definitely concentration camps with which we are concerned in this particular short story.

The world as depicted in a work such as this is essentially the world of tragedy, rooted in the ancient Classical tradition; man, the masses, the elements, woman, and fate. It is restricted to two main protagonists, the hero and his particular interpretation of the meaning of life; those interpersonal conflicts between individuals which endow novels with a more complex thematic structure have no place in this sort of world. Had I intended the Nazis to play as important a role as Kassner does, I would obviously have done so by depicting them more in terms of their true ideological passion: Nationalism.

If we take Flaubert's work, rather than anyone else's, as the most illustrious example of literary values, it completely confuses the issue: Flaubert (who set artistic merit above any other values and, in point of fact, rated the artist higher than saints or heroes) who only created characters with whom he never identified on a personal level, went so far as to write: "I'll drag the whole lot of them through the gutter— it's only fair and I am a fair man". For Aeschylus, as for Corneille, such a notion would have been inconceivable, as it would have been for Hugo, Chateaubriand and even Dostoyevsky. It would have been — and is — accepted by countless authors, so many in fact that even attempting to contradict them would be pointless: we are dealing here with two fundamentally distinct concepts of art. Nietzsche regarded Wagner as having something of the ham actor in him insofar as the latter put so much of his own emotional genius into the portrayal of his characters. Nevertheless, it can be equally valid to predicate the meaning of the word art as being a way of attempting to make men aware of the potential for greatness and nobility of soul they unknowingly possess within themselves.

It is not passion itself, but the desire to prove a point which ruins a work of art; the merit of the latter depends neither upon the degree of emotion nor that of detachment which it portrays, however vividly, but rather upon the compatibility between the subject matter and the means used to express it most effectively. However, if a work's merit — and its "raison d'être", not to mention the duration of its appeal, however short-lived this may be — lies in its *quality*, then whether the author intends it or not, its portrayal of an unusual set of values requires a similar shift of emphasis on the reader's part in his own sensibilities or emotional response to achieve its desired effect; and the work would probably never see the light of day were it not for some hidden need to generate such a mental shift in values. Now it so happens that during the last fifty years or so there has been a change in the history of artistic sensibility in

France which could be called "the agony of virile fraternity". Its true enemy is a kind of confused notion of individualism, which was propagated throughout the nineteenth century and which derived more from a fanatical urge to demonstrate man's differences than from the desire to create a complete, well-rounded individual. This individualism existed too on the part of the artists themselves, who were totally preoccupied with safeguarding "the inner world", an attitude which was justified only when applied to the realm of the emotions or dreams, since the great "Lions of the Renaissance" were clearly always forced to curb their powers of making a point effectively by demonstrating a mulish adherence to traditional values, paying lip-service to the sacred received wisdoms of the age. Moreover, the imposing figure of Caesar Borgia loses something of its glamorous impact when one considers the indisputable fact that most of his obvious power and efficiency derived from the mighty prestige of his backer, the Church. It is common for politicians to be guilty of a contemptuous disregard for their fellow-men, but they keep it firmly under their hats. It is not only during Stendhal's lifetime that the public's prevailing attitudes have forced the true individualist to conceal his real motives and dissemble once he has decided upon a course of action.

The true individual may well oppose collective society, yet it is this very same society which has given him, and nurtured, his set of values. The crucial point here is less a question of knowing what sets him apart from his social group, than discovering from what common source he draws his strength. Like the man of real genius, a true individual's worth lies in his own, particular inner resources. Taking yet another example from the past, the committed Christian led as vital an existence as that of a modern-day individual; having a soul or conscience is surely more valid than being unique, or merely different. Maintaining any kind of psychological existence necessarily involves some form of intellectual barter and the fundamental issue facing someone with positive, concrete values is discovering a means of sustaining those same values, without alienating himself from collective society.

Kassner, like numerous other Communist intellectuals, holds the view that Communism restores to an individual his *fertile mind and resourcefulness*. Whether he is a Roman from the Roman Empire, a Christian, a soldier in the Rhine Army or a Soviet worker, man is intimately bound to the communal society in which he lives; but if he is a devotee of Alexandrines[1] or an eighteenth-century writer, he remains distanced from it. Furthermore, if he is thus distanced from his own society and has no intellectual bond with the following generation, whatever he has to say can in no way be construed as having anything whatsoever to do with heroism. Different human values do exist…

Being a man is difficult. Yet becoming a true individual by exploring what one has in common with one's fellow-men is no more difficult than by consciously cultivating one's difference from others — and the former attitude motivates a man just as powerfully as the latter, if not more so, enabling him to become a real man, to define his humanity. This is the driving force behind his ability to surpass himself, to transcend his human nature, to be creative, or inventive, and which sustains his ability to understand and determine his inner self and values.

[1] See *Notes to the Text*, p. 67.

TO MY GERMAN COMRADES

who urged me to describe

what they had endured and

what they had managed to

preserve.

THIS BOOK IS FOR THEM

CHAPTER I

Kassner was shoved into the guardroom just as a prisoner they were interrogating was finishing a sentence, but his words were drowned out by the usual police-station racket of rustling papers and clumping boots. Facing him on the other side of the table was a typical Hitlerite official: with the familiar square-jowled, angular face and virtually shaven head, his hair closely cropped from the ears up, and with short, blond tufts sticking up stiffly from his skull.

"... Party orders!".

"Since when?"

"1924."

"What post did you hold in the illegal Communist party?"

"I don't know anything about any illegal party. Until January 1933 my duties in the German party were of a purely technical nature."

The Communist shifted slightly, almost turning his back on Kassner, and the latter had to listen closely to their voices to be able to tell who was talking. The prisoner was speaking in a low, impersonal voice, as if he were deliberately using such a tone to show that it was not *he*, himself, who was answering, but someone else who was being forced to reply under duress and was not responsible for his actions. The interrogator's voice sounded detached, even younger than his youthful looks suggested. As he listened, Kassner waited for something in the voice and words which would gradually give him an insight into the character of this young man who was to be responsible for his fate.

The latter was looking at the prisoner, who was looking into space.

"You've been to Russia."

"As a technician: I was working for the Electrozavod."[2]

"We'll look into that. What post did you hold in the German Volga Republic?"[3]

"Never been to any such Republic. Nor to the Volga."

"What cell[4] did you belong to in Berlin?"

"Ex-1015."

"We'll see. Who was your leader?"

The Communist's back was completely turned towards him now, and Kassner listened for his reply.

"Hans."

"I knew it. I want his surname! Are you making fun of me, arse-hole?"

"We only ever knew our comrades by their first names. It was always like that, whoever it was."

"His address?"

"I only ever saw him at the cell."

"All right. Well, I'm going to put you in one of ours: you'll see how that will improve your memory. How long were you at Moabit?"[5]

"Six months."

"One hundred and eighty days after your arrest...?"

Kassner finally began thinking about his own arrest. The SA[6] had taken him off in a bus to begin with, (which, because its passengers were all Nazis, seemed even more stifling than a prison van). One of the businesses he was supposed to be running was a small factory which made adjustable airscrews, which meant that, from time to time, he was officially permitted to use a plane. The latter was lying dormant now, out there in its hangar and, for the whole journey, it had been the only thing Kassner could think about. On one of the street corners some men were singing while they were repainting an ironmonger's shop-front — its gaudy colours reminded him of the Red Square... Until then, everything had seemed unreal to him, more like a ritual than a dream.

"One hundred and eighty..." the interrogator resumed. "Well, well... So who's been sleeping with your wife all this time?"

Had the prisoner given any hint that the blow had struck home, while the other man had been staring at him so intently? Kassner was intensely aware of the prisoner's unwilling presence, stuck there physically captive, yet striving hard to remain mentally detached from what was happening. The interrogator softened his tone, less aggressive now.

"Who's sleeping with your wife then?" he repeated.

Kassner put himself in the Communist's shoes, feeling somehow like a spectator and a tragic actor at one and the same time and could not think straight any more.

"I'm not married," the prisoner replied, shifting sideways again.

Another pause.

"That doesn't mean you can't have a woman...," the Nazi finally replied, in the same indifferent tone of voice.

The two men stared at one another with weary disgust.

The official jerked his chin: two SA men led the prisoner away, then pushed Kassner towards the table. The Nazi looked at him, opened a dossier and took out a photo.

Like anyone who has ever needed to conceal their identity from time to time, every single feature of his own horsy elongated face, with its square-set jaws, was permanently imprinted on Kassner's memory. Which photo was the Hitlerite scrutinising? Kassner could see it upside-down from where he was. Not much danger there: he'd had a short back and sides at the time it had been taken and the expression on that narrow, bony mask-like face, with its pointed ears, was passably different from the way he looked now, with his longish brown hair framing a haggard, thoroughbred face, giving him a vaguely romantic look. The photo had been taken when he'd had his mouth tightly closed; he knew that the minute he smiled his long teeth were exposed right down to the gums. Even when he was just biting his lower lip those teeth were still very obvious. He did so now — but only slightly, because one of his molars was hurting him, — and dropped his gaze towards the table: usually his very large eyes appeared to be looking slightly more upwards than is natural and in order to conceal the white line which normally showed between his irises and lower lids he only needed to appear to be looking downwards.

Silently, the Nazi stared first at the photo then at the face, in turn. Kassner knew that if he were recognised, he would be killed, whether or not he was officially condemned to death.

"Kassner," said the Nazi.

Every single clerk and SA man looked up suddenly.

It was the first time Kassner had witnessed recognition of his legend written on enemy faces.

"I'm well-known at my legation. Even the dumbest conspirator wouldn't ask a policeman for a light only to walk straight into a police ambush."

He'd been with some comrades in a small antique shop belonging to one of them, half an hour before going to a dentist's appointment, when a member of the illegal organisation had come in, hung his overcoat above a pile of Dalmatian vestments, icons, chasubles and orthodox bric-à-brac and sat down, saying: "There's a police-ambush at Wolf's. They're going to take people in for questioning." Wolf had stood up. "I've got a list of names in the back of my watch-case."

They'd been told never to keep any names at home.

"You'll be arrested at the entrance. Where's the watch?" "In the wardrobe, in the pocket of my black waistcoat. But it's..." "Don't argue: the list! Give me the keys." When he'd arrived there Kassner had met two SA men in the corridor: it hadn't exactly been an ambush. He'd stopped in front of them and tried to light the cigarette he'd already got between his lips with an empty lighter. He'd asked the SA men for a light and gone upstairs. While he was ringing the doorbell he'd leant against the door to hide his hand which was pushing the key into the keyhole, gone in, closed the door behind him, opened the wardrobe, taken out the watch, eaten the list, put the watch back and closed the wardrobe door again. No sound of footsteps on the stairs. He knew he'd be arrested when he went downstairs. There was nowhere to hide the key in the room and opening the window to throw it out would have been absolutely stupid. He'd slid the key into the pocket of one of the pairs of trousers hanging in the wardrobe: Wolf could have had several keys.

He'd had to wait for five minutes, to make it seem as if he'd come to see Wolf and had not found him at home. The taste of the paper he was chewing with some discomfort (was it a nerve or a bad tooth? If only all this could have happened after the dentist's!) reminded him of the smell of papier-mâché carnival masks. Even if all went well, it was going to be difficult to get out of this place: false identity-papers are only worth so much... And the prospect of Nazi prisons did not exactly fill him with enthusiasm. Who really knows just how much they can endure? How many times had he been told that, even by trying to obtain one extra ration, a prisoner will end up expending the same amount of energy as what would be spent on setting up an illegal organisation covering an entire district? He'd thrown away his cigarette: the taste of the tobacco combined with the chewed paper made him feel sick. He'd finally gone out and they had arrested him on the landing.

"You will find more than fifteen letters at my factory — evidence of the correspondence between Mr Wolf and ourselves, as you may see for yourselves," said Kassner. "All the stock has been delivered."

The illegal organisation had taken all possible precautions.

His Pilsen accent was not bad, but the real Kassner was from Munich. While he had been working as a militant Kassner had developed an almost unconscious habit of using the rhetorical phrase "as you may see" quite frequently. He found it extremely repugnant using such a deferential expression when talking to Nazis, and — although it was virtually useless — he had had to watch himself and speak more slowly. Both an interrogator and the man he is interrogating know just how difficult it is to prove that a meticulously established false identity is in fact a fake. The Nazi flicked through the dossier, looked up, then started flicking through it again.

Photo, thought Kassner, description. But what are all those papers? The SA man had confirmed that Kassner had asked him for a light. But how had he got in? They hadn't found the key on him, so that was all right, and they'd heard him ringing the doorbell; but if they'd known that the door was unlocked...

What picture of his life did these bits of paper conjure up? A miner's son; a University student on a grant and organiser of one of the workers' theatres; he had been imprisoned by the Russians, then gone over to the partisans and then joined the Red Army; he had been a party delegate in China and Mongolia; he was a writer who had returned to Germany in 1932 to organise the Rühr strikes against Papen's decree,[7] he ran the illegal information service, was a former vice-president of the "Red Relief"[8]... Clearly enough to get him executed, but consistent with someone who had a rather haughty expression.

"It's one thing getting into the Legation with false papers but quite another going out in the street with them on you," observed the Nazi.

But Kassner sensed him hesitate. Everyone around him hesitated: people expect somebody who has led a fantastically romantic life to at least look the part. It seemed that Kassner, the columnist who had chronicled the Siberian Civil War,[9] who was blessed with an extremely impressive physique enhanced by his contacts with the theatre, and with a raw genius for expressing virile emotion, ought to bear visible signs of all the dramas he had witnessed and described, because his life had become merged in people's memories with the messy Siberian epic. Besides, it was a well-known fact that he had been in Germany since Hitler's triumph, and was held in great affection by all those people who had been defeated, who saw him as both their comrade-in-arms (his job was important, but not crucially so), and the future historian of their time of overwhelming despair. Even his enemies believed that he had become involved in the events he had witnessed, like the traveller who returns home visibly marked by his experiences in the countries he has journeyed through, or like the passer-by who has narrowly escaped being caught up in a catastrophe. Everyone expected to see a face that bore visible signs of the Siberian experience; not so long ago they would probably have seen those ravaged features in the photos of him published in the newspapers, where it would have been easy to touch them up like that. It was not quite so easy to modify the features of a living person in such a way. Almost to a man, those who were hesitating now felt it was ridiculous that this man should have been taken for Kassner. The interrogator left the room, came back, closed his dossier again and made the same sign with his chin as he had at the end of the previous cross-examination. Two SA men pushed Kassner towards the door and, manhandling and thumping him (although without really exceeding the limits of conventional military brutality) propelled him towards the prison.

If they'd been going to finish me off right away, they'd have taken me to the guardhouse, thought Kassner.

But they weren't going to: corridors, and more corridors. Finally he was locked up in a rather large, dark hole.

A quarter of an hour later, the darkness gradually receded into the grey- painted walls which began to emerge from the gloom. Kassner roamed aimlessly around his cell, his mind a blank. Realising this, he pulled himself together and stopped. The wall was dirtier nearer the door and lower down, near the floor. Was it like that because other people had roamed around here, as he was doing now? There was no sign of dust anywhere though. The cell looked clean in a Germanic way —hygienically clean. Was it dampness? He realised that by now he was mechanically going through a list of questions: while his mind, like his stupid body, was roaming around restlessly (I must be looking more and more like a horse), his gaze had frozen, his eyes registering the fact quicker than his brain: low down, near its base, the wall was covered with inscriptions. His mind was latching on to anything within its grasp, avoiding having to think about his imprisonment. What could he think about? Now he'd been recognised, all he needed to know was whether they would turn up soon and finish him off, or torture him or just beat him up; might as well think about the graffiti on the wall.

Several bits were only half-visible. Some were coded. (If I'm going to stay here, I'll work out the code). Others were much clearer. Very slowly this time, he began to roam about the cell again, focusing on the more obvious, distinct ones and as he approached them he made out: *I don't want...* The rest was obliterated. Another one: *Dying in the street would have been less terrible than dying here.* Several times since he had been captured, Kassner had told himself that having a real fight on their hands would have helped them win over the majority of the workers who were not on their side; but he knew how his romantic imagination so easily ran away with him and was extremely wary of this tendency of his. "We can never win if we only have the progressives on our side," ran an obsessively memorable sentence of Lenin's. Ever since he had returned to Germany, Kassner had felt instinctively that it was impossible to unite all the workers in a single body without infiltrating the Catholic, reformist unions, and they had not been able to do enough effective work among the unions to persuade the other workers to become involved in the struggle: the revolutionary workers had been the first to be sacked and had become artisans, with the result that barely one tenth of the party was carrying on the campaign inside the large factories. During the previous year, there had been fewer strikes in Germany than in France, England or the United States... Kassner had been working on organising the Red unions: they had got more than three hundred thousand members by the end of the year... but that was still not enough.

Now that Hitler was in power, all the various revolutionary factions within the factories needed to pull together and form one single union which would militate in a more focused manner. It would then pull in one direction only, targeting the campaign into reacting immediately to more rapidly reported daily events and, being in closer contact with the core organisations, it would then be able to implement instructions from base much more effectively. As a result, Kassner had been working at the information service centre since January; this was one of the most risky jobs and most of the more legible inscriptions — the most recent ones — had almost certainly been scratched on that wall by some of its members. He bent towards another one: *My hair is still black,* and, as if his choice of message had been dictated by some acute instinct of his, more accurate than his eyes even, his ears picked up the distinct sound of footsteps. Were there many of them?

The sounds were all jumbled up: there must have been three, four, at least five, maybe six of them out there.

Six SA guards could only be coming along here — a whole group of them, at this hour — to beat somebody up.

The door of a distant cell was opened then closed again, the woolly silence once more engulfing the commotion caused by the clumping boots.

The real threat wasn't pain, nor being killed: no — the real threat was the ingenious sadism of those men who'd just gone in and shut that door. Anywhere in the world, the kind of people who choose that career are the lowest of the low.

When you get down to basics, when it's a question of real humiliation, just like with real pain, it's always the torturer who is most likely to be the strongest — not the victim. "If they tortured me to try to get information that I haven't got out of me, I couldn't take it. Let's imagine I don't have any," he thought aloud. At this point he started channelling his mind and courage into becoming detached from his inner self, separating the person who in a few minutes' time would be at the mercy of the sound of those menacing boots, from the real Kassner he would revert to being later.

There was such an oppressive atmosphere inside the prison that even the guards spoke to each other in hushed tones. Suddenly, the sound of a long drawn-out scream filled his cell, lasting until it was choked off and finally stifled.

Better become completely passive, and escape into a world of blissfully irresponsible sleep and madness; yet somehow keep enough of one's wits about one to be on the defensive and not let oneself be completely and utterly destroyed in here. Better become totally detached rather than let them get anything but the bare essentials out of one.

The shrieking started again. More piercing this time. Kassner stuck his fingers in his ears. Useless: his mind had already synchronised with the rhythm of that agonised cry of pain, so that when the next shriek came he was already expecting it.

He was used to war by now but he had never, ever, heard a man being tortured and screaming in a confined place. The war-wounded might groan, but their anguished moans were nothing like this, which was all the more terrifying because he didn't know what had caused it. What kind of torture was being inflicted on that man to make him scream like that; what was he himself going to be forced to endure, soon? Being tortured out in the open air suddenly seemed infinitely preferable to him — a favour even.

The door closed again, the footsteps came towards his cell.

He became aware that he was pinned, shoulders hunched, against the wall of his den. He might well have summoned up his own will but his knees certainly hadn't summoned up theirs. He drew away from the wall, exasperated by his limp legs.

A second door closed behind the footsteps, as if it had caught them on the move. Silence reigned once more over an ants' nest of tiny scrabbling sounds.

He went back towards the door: *Stahl killed on the...* The inscription was unfinished, but not rubbed out this time; the wall oozed with men's destinies.

He remembered seeing a letter that had been written by a prisoner's wife: "He'd been so battered and beaten! I didn't recognise him, Thérèse, I couldn't pick him out from the others..."

How many of his own people would be stuck in here after him? They still hadn't taken his pencil away from him. *We are with you,* he wrote.

As he drew back his hand he noticed another inscription: *I'm going to kill Federwisch before the end of the month.* Federwisch was one of the camp's former commanders. Which of the two was now dead, the man who had written that threat or the man he had sworn to kill?

While he was glancing through the rows of graffiti, his straining ears picked up the sound of guards' footsteps and a vague scratching sound coming from neighbouring cells, and even the noise of a shouting match going on in a yard somewhere in the distance... the sound echoing along the corridors in a strangely hushed way yet at the same time distinctly audible... No more screams yet. He began to feel he was living in a world which consisted entirely of sounds and threatening noises, the world of a blind man in danger.

He knew how difficult it is not to meet force with force when you are being beaten up. He was not unaware of his own physical strength, of that masculine lack of restraint which had so often enabled him to penetrate to the numbed inner world of men's hearts where memories of their dead loved ones lay buried; but opening up, himself, and talking to the Nazis was the last thing he wanted to do. Besides, the more impartial, less fanatical Hitlerites had not exactly chosen to be slave-guards. Kassner knew only too well that, even though any man is capable of killing another man in a fight, if you beat up a prisoner you will end up needing one of those contemptible State pardons. All he needed to do was to manage to remain silent. He did not need to counter any physical assaults by making historic declarations, he needed to escape so that he could get back to his work as a revolutionary again. Maybe they would beat him up; but, at Hagen,[10] it had been impossible to get any one person from a factory of seven hundred and fifty workers, to denounce a single one of the people who had been distributing pamphlets, despite all the terrorising they had endured.

"You'll see how this will change your memories for ever..."

He stood there, stock still in the middle of his cell, elbows pinned to his sides, waiting for another scream. Nothing. Yet, because the cell the SA men had just gone into was nearer his than the first one, he thought that he could hear the sound of muffled blows... Eventually, while he was still bracing himself for another shriek, he caught the sound of a low yelping, distinctly audible between the two metallic clicks of a door opening and closing.

Footsteps echoed again, much nearer this time. Kassner moved across his cell towards the door, which opened just as he reached it.

Four SA men came in, while two remained in the corridor. There they stood, arms stiffly hooped in front of them, heads jutting forward — their faces illuminated by the light of a hurricane-lamp one of them had placed on the floor.

While they'd still been invisible, and faceless and bodiless as far as he was concerned, they'd seemed infinitely more terrifying than these blokes who, at that instant, looked like caricatures of male strength with their arms sticking out from their shoulders, rather like Hercules and the chimpanzees. His feeling of terror subsided. His fears had been instinctive, primitive, a mixture of suffering and fear of the unknown; he'd probably been expecting a sadist, a drunk or a madman —something inhuman, more than anything else. These blokes were not drunk. They could still be sadists though. But since they'd been standing there, his fears had already given way to feelings of exaltation and resolute self-confidence.

They were looking at him. They probably could not see him very clearly, just as he could barely make out their shapeless forms, with only their chins and cheekbones lit from below and their squat, shadowy silhouettes weaving around on the ceiling above them like gigantic spiders. For the second time, he felt as though he were trapped in a den, with every single stone of the prison building piled up around the entrance to his hollow. The flickering light was also illuminating his own cheekbones from below. It felt painful; no, of course, it was because he was clenching his teeth with all his might. Bitterly, he suddenly realised that his tooth wasn't hurting him any longer. He resolved not to give an inch.

A sudden, sharp blow to his stomach bent him double, jack-knifing his body as if he had caved in on himself; another punch smashed into his chin as his head fell forward, sending him reeling backwards. As he fell, the cement floor got him in his ribs which were also being hammered by the guards' flailing boots. Although he was on the verge of passing out completely, he was stunned by the fact that he did not feel in any great pain; compared with the torture and everything else he had been expecting, being only punched and kicked around was absolutely ridiculous. Anyway, the vulnerable softer parts of his body were protected because he had rolled over onto his stomach. It seemed that his ribs and bones were forming a protective cage around his stomach, shielding him from the relentless kicking. A blow to his jaw brought blood oozing from his mouth, he could feel it trickling down and, at the very instant he heard someone say: "So, you're spitting out your flag then?", a blinding red flash burst in front of his eyes: a neck chop. He eventually lost consciousness.

He vaguely sensed being flung into another cell and hearing someone shout: "See you soon."

As the cell door shut, he felt a wave of comfort flow over him, at first. This door might be closing him in but it did protect him from the horrific indignities and lunacy which reigned outside. At the same time, the solitude, the sense of his own powerlessness and the slow regaining of his consciousness took him back to those inner fears of childhood and the apprehension he had experienced when he used to play at being a wild beast, crouching underneath tables. He felt nothing but relief.

How long to go before dawn? A guard briefly opened and shut a spyhole in the door. As he did so the light from the corridor fell on the far wall of Kassner's cell and he could see a grille set into it which seemed to be covering a narrow ventilation-hole as deep as a slit in a fortress's battlements. This hole in the wall did not link his cell to the living world after all. He was living in a totally autonomous and suffocating world; the hole only made one realise even more just how crushingly thick the stonework was. Kassner was in a tomb, as cut-off from the world as if he were asleep or mad, while that hole made the suffocatingly thick, pitted stone seem like the shell of a live carapace under which those prisoners who could still walk scuttled about incessantly like tireless millipedes.

He felt around for the wall and knocked on it with his bent fore-finger — just giving a few knocks — leaving an interval between each one. No reply.

Kassner's exhilaration had evaporated since his beating. The initial feeling of euphoria which had buoyed him up when they had closed his cell door was now degenerating into anxiety: it was ebbing away from him in waves, like shreds of tattered clothing, away from his sensitive skin, and even from his clothes which had become as limp as nightwear. They had ripped off his braces and shoelaces (so suicide wasn't going to be an option then), and cut off his buttons, so that the very material of his clothing seemed to have been transformed. Was it that hole, or was it the pain which was gradually boring through his feverishness, or was it the darkness that was making him feel so oppressed? Condemned men who are locked up in solitary confinement, in round cells where there is nothing to focus on, always go mad.

He knocked on the wall again.

The two right-angled strips of light which were still outlining the door went out.

His strength began to eat away at him persistently, like a gnawing parasite. He was a man of action by nature, and the gloom was sapping his energy and willpower.

He had to bide his time. That was all. He had to sit it out. He had to lie low and be vigilant, as vigilant as paralysed people are, or like mourners surrounding the dying. His stubborn will-power would be entombed in there with him, keeping a vigil alongside him like a dim, watchful face hanging, disembodied, out there in the depths of the shadows.

Otherwise, he really would go insane.

CHAPTER II

How many days had it been?

It was pitch dark, apart from the occasional crack of light showing between the door and the door-jamb, and the patrols doing their rounds. How many days had he been there, alone, growing madder by the minute and croaking away feebly like a toad?

The thrashings and beatings were still going on in the cells all around him.

Maybe it was daytime outside. Real daytime filled with trees and grass and towns, their zinc-clad roofs glowing, blue-tinged, in the early morning light...

Although his wife was in Prague, for the last twenty minutes he had been convinced that she had died. Died while he was shut away in here, locked in like a pet animal. He could see her deceptively mulatto-like face, its features as serene as a dead person's, her over-full lips now slightly more tightly closed. Her wavy hair was all over the place, her eyelids half-closed over her enormous, pale-blue eyes, eyes like a Siamese cat's, and her mask-like expression now relieved of pain and devoid of joy — its former vivaciousness utterly drained away. Even if he ever succeeded in getting away from here, once he got out he would return to a world which would be forever cut off from the old one; he would bear the scars of that lonely death for the rest of his life. This alone was enough to make him realise what a powerful effect the darkness was having on him, tying his mind up in knots, and how powerful was the enemy which had succeeded in cutting him off like this from the solid reality of the real world, just like the insane or the dead.

The guards' footsteps went away, echoing dully along the corridor, the muffled repetitive tread sounding as monotonous as anything connected with death-marches or funerals always does. "If I can do ten rounds of the cell before the second guard comes along — (they followed each other in succession at fairly regular intervals) — she might still be alive after all," he mumbled aloud.

He started pacing round. Two. Three. He bumped into the wall which he had thought was further away. Four. "I shouldn't be going so fast. I should be going at a steadier pace." He was acutely aware that he was limping as he tore around. Six. The guard's footsteps rang out again. Seven. Eight. This time he shot around, making such a tight turn he almost tripped up. The guard went past.

Nine.

He lay down on the ground. Lying on the floor was forbidden. "If I've counted up to a hundred before they come back, she's alive," he mumbled. One, two, three... Silence. His eyes were closed, the numbers were totting up, one after the other, as they do before an execution. Sixty, eighty, ninety-eight, one hundred: "She's alive."

He saw Anna's eyes open and opened his own: while he had been counting, he had unconsciously drawn his feet together and crossed his arms over his chest like a corpse.

"I'm already going insane," he thought.

He heard the sound of the guards' footsteps again, but decided not to get up: he wanted to see another human being. His own brand of bravery was like any other person's, he found it far easier to summon up his courage and use it more effectively when confronting actual danger than when facing his inner fears. He had been aware of this since a night in Siberia, in a village which could have been surrounded by the Whites[11] at any time; he had felt fear gripping him then, but once he had thought of opening the doors and windows of his *isba*,[12] he had fallen asleep.

The guards went past without opening the spy-hole. "It's hard trying to finish oneself off in here before... I really must make something up. If they torture me, if I'm lucky I might be able to keep my mouth shut, but if I go mad... I can't have saved the list only to go and give away things which are ten times more important than that was! Maybe one doesn't notice..." Perhaps people are unaware when they are drifting into madness, perhaps this was a rare moment of lucidity now, when he realised he was in his cell, trying to save his wife's life by counting out numbers and lying corpse-like on the floor.

A guard came back along the corridor, humming a tune to himself. Music!

There was nothing here, nothing around him but a geometrically-shaped hollow in the immense mass of stone and nothing in that but human flesh waiting to be tortured. But there would be Russian songs, and Bach and Beethoven too, inside this hole. His memory was full of them.

Slowly, very slowly, the music began to drive away his madness, lifting it from his breast, then from his arms, then from his fingers and out of his cell; it gently stroked every one of his muscles, with the exception of his incredibly tender throat (although he was not actually singing out loud, he was only remembering the music) which felt as tender as his split lower lip. Rising, then falling away and then swelling again with lyrical abandon, the dreamy, imaginary sounds filled his mind, bringing back memories of love and childhood feelings, of all those human emotions that well up and make men choke in their throats: sometimes breaking down into sobbing or crying or even panic. Now, slowly stealing into the brooding silence of Kassner's surroundings, as silent as the hush before a storm, and rising above his enslavement and madness, above his dead wife and child, above his dead friends and above the whole host of terrified people, rose a soft but sublimely musical expression of all mankind's joy and grief.

He began to feel disturbing waves of numbness radiating outwards from behind his closed eyelids, rather like his wounds which, little by little, were being slowly deadened by the increasingly oppressive, solemn quiet of the empty space around him. Suddenly, as if a hand had brushed past, flattening the vast forest of sounds, the melody died away then soared aloft once more, tearing at each of his wounds, raising him afloat like a vessel and carrying him to the very extremes of pain with its passionate tide: bewitching music which, as ever, personifies the lusty appeal of love. Madness was lying in wait there, beneath his pain-wracked consciousness, taking cover in his limbs, waiting to ambush him in the same way the pain had since he had stopped moving around. He was becoming more and more obsessed by a nightmare in which he was locked in a cage with a vulture which, using its beak like a pick-axe, was tearing off bits of his skin each time it pecked him while its beady eyes were constantly fixed on his own in a steady, covetous gaze. The vulture edged nearer, swollen and grotesque after hours of gorging on the black blood of darkness but the music out-matched it, triumphant. It overwhelmed Kassner and took possession of his senses.

Gelsenkirchen[13] is ice-bound: a dog is barking at a flight of wild ducks on the wing, the sound dying out in the spikily quiet, icy intimacy of the snow; loud-hailers calling for strikes are competing with the mines' sirens; sunflowers, their yellow petals crushed and bloodstained, lying strewn out, flattened by the partisans' fighting. Wintertime in a Mongolia grown lividly pale within only three days, where crushed, dried-up rose petals drift like dead butterflies in the dusty yellow wind; frogs croaking in the rainy dawn of a village where the palm-trees have withered, the rebel lorries' horns honking away even during the night; the castanet-like clicketing sound of Chinese merchants fleeing before the Red Lancers[14] and disappearing beneath the glow-worms at the end of a palm-fringed path. The Yangtze River is in full flood, its waters spreading interminably into the distance, corpses banked up against the fallen trees, hooked on their claw-like stumps, the whole scene bathed in deathly pale moonlight; and all those heads flattened against the freezing, insect-infested ground, listening for the rumbling sound of the White Army somewhere out there on the distant steppes or Mongolian plains. The memories of his youth, together with his pain and even his very will-power — everything — began slowly revolving round and round in his mind and, with the imperceptible but inexorable pace of a celestial galaxy, gravitated slowly towards oblivion.

Vulture and prison-cell now disappeared, submerged beneath a ferocious cascade of funereal chanting, blended indistinguishably together in a relentless tide of sound in which the music transformed any remaining vestige of the past into an eternal present devoid of any sense of time, consigning it all to its collective memory just as life and death merge into oblivion in the stillness of the star-studded heavens. Tattered war-torn landscapes, women's voices, fleeing shadows, every last shred of his memories dissolved into a constant, continuous deluge which spilled down onto everything as if its relentless downpour would sweep it all back into the depths of time past.

Perhaps death itself was like this music: whether it occurred in this very place, or in the guard-room or even in the cellar: perhaps, at the very moment one was being killed one's life, his life, would stretch out before him, devoid of any hatred or violence, totally submerged in a sea of solemn calm as his body felt now in this sea of darkness, as if his woolly patchwork of memories were being swamped by the sacred chorus.

Somewhere out there, beyond his cell, beyond time itself, an undefeated if pain-wracked world did exist, a twilight world scoured with primitive raw emotions, where the whole of what had been his former life was moving inexorably onward, like those myriad other worlds making their steady, unerring progress through the heavens, and slipping imperceptibly into an everlastingly conscious reflection of eternity. Just as when his mind had spread its wings and soared away into a world of dreams, it now swept down like a billowing, wind-filled sail and, little by little, totally confused by now, he felt his thin, spare body synchronising with the inevitable, eternal march of the stars, fascinated by this army of the night, drifting away through a world of total silence towards eternity. Mongolian skies above the Tartar camel-train drivers sprawling prostrate out in the dusty Gobi desert[15] amid the smell of withered jasmine, their chanting cut off by the evening psalm: *and if this night should be one of destiny — Blessed be that night till dawn appears...*

He stood up. As soon as he remained still for a while, his limbs and skin seemed to dissolve in the gloom. He could only feel the most acutely painful places, concentrated nodules of pain, like dense knots in wood grain, when he actually moved. The minute he took a step forward he rediscovered his body's framework, with its bones and its aching, throbbing joints and his head, which seemed larger in the dark than it had during the daytime. Yet there was something other in the music than simply its fatal ability to take over a man's mind with its compelling melodies, bringing about its complete and utter breakdown, and sending him drifting off, ever more blissfully, into a lost world of comforting numbness. Rising from the depths of the underworld, surging up and echoing insistently, came a call to arms, a communal appeal from the revolutionary host that peopled the Valley of the Last Judgment. A world now in full revolt and in which music gently embraces a man's head, slowly raising it to join the virile brotherhood of man, uniting with the appeals of those who, at this very moment, were daubing the red insignia on something somewhere and calling for vengeance upon the houses of their massacred comrades, of those who were replacing the names on street-signs with the names of their friends who had been tortured, of those men in Essen, who had been repeatedly clubbed until, as limp as if they had been strangled, they fell to the ground and lay face down in the blood which poured from their mouths and noses. All because the SA had wanted to make them sing the *Internationale* and, there on the ground, they had yelled it at their torturers in tones of such savage hope that the N.C.O. had grabbed his gun and fired at them.

Shaken by the hymn, Kassner lurched forward in spite of himself, rather like a shattered skeleton. But now, hard upon another haunting memory which the voices had conjured up in his mind, despite the profoundly morbid recollections they had initially triggered off, loomed the memory of a hundred thousand men singing revolutionary songs in a rousing chorus (and there is nothing more exhilarating in music than a resounding phrase, sung out by a multitude of men in total unison), the lusty chorus ebbing and flowing over the heads of the crowd like the shimmering patterns traced by the wind across immense wheatfields, right to the horizon. Now yet another chant seemed to be luring everything into never-ending oblivion with its compellingly solemn rhythm; and, at long last, amid the same still, utter calm that enfolds a dead and buried army, the music transcended its heroic appeals just as it transcends everything, just as it is in its very nature to overcome everything, to consume all it touches with its intricate tongues of fire, like a burning bush quietly going up in flames. Night was closing in across the whole universe, night-time during which, whether they are on the move or just together in total silence, men were communicating with each other; wanton night-time, pregnant with stars and expectant friendship... Fluttering like his own exhausted masculine heart was doing now, the night's uncertain rhythm pulsated apprehensively, beating time with each moment of his youth, with the strikes in the mines, with the barking which echoed from farm to farm across the fields, slowly awakening the sleeping cows; and, when the chorus had died away completely, the ardent pathos of life and death, which had earlier fused together in musical harmony, foundered upon mankind's infinite, eternal bondage. The stars would inevitably travel through the same parts of the twinkling heavens on their predestined course, and those captive stars would forever roam around that vast limbo, like those captive prisoners in the yard outside, like him here in his cell. Now, as a note rang out three times in succession, like bells pealing, its first note painfully reverberating through every single one of his wounds, the last remaining shreds of the tattered star-studded heavens receded into the depths of that world of terror and, little by little, reassembled and turned into the shape of a vulture.

He waited, eyes tightly shut, his hands shaking slightly now as he feverishly clutched at his chest. Nothing. There was nothing here but the gigantic all-enveloping mass of stonework on all sides and that other kind of night, the deathly darkness of dead of night. He was pressed against the wall. "Like a millipede," he thought, listening to that world of music his mind had conjured up and which was slowly ebbing away, beaching him there like a dead fish, and flowing off back into nothingness, taking with it the ringing sounds of human joy.

The only kind of man who could ever reconcile himself to living with that mass of stone all around him would have to be a secretive and repressed sub-human being who had ended up losing all track of time. For the prisoners who were locked up in their cells, time was like a giant black spider that was swinging to and fro above their heads, every bit as mesmerising and ghastly for them as time was for their comrades who were also locked up, but condemned to death. In Kassner's case he was suffering not so much because of his present predicament but rather from an obsession with the future, a feeling that whatever happened would be perpetuated "forever". It was neither the cold, nor the darkness nor the suffocating mass of solid stone that was weighing him down and transfixing his mind so powerfully, it was the locked door of his cell and his feeling of total dependence on forces beyond his control.

Somewhere inside his mind, something was trying to make him adapt himself to his present situation and the only way to do this was to relapse into a state of suspended animation — a sort of dazed numbness punctuated by the long musical melodies which had hung behind, laggard-like, in his cell. These melodies were in fact phrases of Orthodox plain-chant which, with their virtually static rhythm, were hauntingly reminiscent of that dreadful moment when he had decided to let himself be arrested. Once again, they brought back memories of the Russian bric-à-brac in the antique collector's shop, with all its icons, mantles, albs, chasubles, togas and crosses, and then eventually faded away into the soundless void. Kassner began slowing down mentally to cope with having to live out the fight against both his torpor and the glutinously slow dragging-past of time, obsessed by images of Russian gold-plate which lay as deep in the recesses of his haunted mind as if they were lying in the depths of a sunken galley's hulk. He felt that he would go on re-enacting this struggle until the end of time, pacing himself ever more slowly and spacing the bad moments out at ever-increasing intervals, like ripples spreading outwards on the surface of water, until everything finally became dissipated in the crushing silence of complete and utter mental exhaustion.

Someone was knocking. Were they knocking on the door of his cell?

He'd been expecting to hear that sound ever since he'd been in his cell.

The knocking came again.

"Who is it?" he asked.

Low, but unmistakably real, voices answered from the other side of the door: "It's us". They were not standing there arms akimbo this time, they were standing there stock-still like a delegation of emotionally detached ambassadors with its hushed fateful pronouncements sent by Torture itself. But the knocking went on: five knocks — then another two; each knock bringing Kassner gradually back to whatever level of consciousness could possibly be retrieved from that gloom: it was another prisoner knocking.

Two knocks, a pause, then six more; then a longer pause.

Nobody had answered his own tapping. It would be absolutely insane to even begin to hope.

Wasn't it just as mad though, to shun even the slightest hope?

Five knocks; two; two, six; nine; ten; one, four; one, four; two, six; nine.

He was already getting it all muddled up. That Orthodox plain-chant, that sepulchral chanting rising above a cathedral's plundered treasures; that was making it all worse and making the coded numbers even more muddled as well! Firstly though, first: he'd got to let them know he was listening! He knocked on the wall. The other person would reply, and would obviously repeat his message.

How could one write anything down in a cell?

The other prisoner started knocking again, more slowly this time.

How can I write, how on earth can I write down something? Kassner felt like stamping on the ground, like a horse stamping its hoof, the next time he heard the knocking start again and stamping along with every knock with all his might; but even so, that would not help him remember the sequence properly. "I'll have to think about this." How on earth could one think when one's whole body was being transfixed by an acute awareness of that elusive presence, by waiting for the knocking to start again and by that sound of enraged despair which was actually the sound of his teeth chattering?

The other man began knocking again.

5, 2; 2, 6; 9; 10; 1, 4; 1, 4; 2, 6; 9.

And the chanting was still going on.

"What was it they called torture by hope?"... If he, Kassner, sent a message in his turn, maybe the other man could note down what he said. But how could one work out an alphabet? The knocking was going to start again soon...

Trying to think clearly and concentrate was one of the greatest efforts he had ever made in the whole of his life. He could not get the picture of a raised hand just missing a passing fly out of his mind. However, he did manage to take in the fact that the other man was tapping out thirteen numbers. If I could reduce them to a single number, maybe I'd remember it. No. Too long. How about halving it? Maybe... Silence.

He waited, scarcely able to breathe, his entire body convulsed by his feverish efforts. He tried rapping again, at random now, making no attempt at coding whatsoever. Nothing. He hadn't gone deaf: he could hear himself knocking and walking round, and he could still hear the confused rumble of all the goings-on in the prison above the persistent drone of the religious chanting going on in his head. The guards had opened a nearby door. Had they just caught the man who had been knocking on the wall or had they simply happened to order him outside his cell? His hopes faded, just as the music had done earlier, plunging him once more into a numbed daze. Yet he still managed to keep straining his ears just in case the knocking would start again. But in vain, and his last remaining false hopes drained away like the last deceptive oozing of blood from a mortal wound, when a heart is still beating before its pulsing rhythm is finally checked.

He shut his eyes, succombing to the silent, dazed world of semi-wakefulness. He was just conscious of a series of jumbled images flashing through his mind, through which he vaguely made out that the first one was a kind of iridescence, resembling petrol mixed with water; it finally resolved itself into a pink colour shot through with black marks, which looked like circumflex accents. Was it that place on the river where the White Army's exploding shells had scattered the stunned, suffocated fish all over the starving soldiers who were holding their guns cocked in a T position while clusters of pink-bellied fish glinted in the shimmering, salmon-tinged cold light of dawn?... Then, as if all of a sudden the sun had risen, the glittering pink hues merged into gold and turned into a lavish display of religious gold-plate similar to the antique shop's collection of ornaments. Their embossments were flickering amid the chanting going on, making them look like the tiny votive lamps in front of icons, yet at the same time they were the side-lamps of the Trans-Siberian train lying motionless, stranded in the forest beneath the telegraph poles, like a ship that has run aground.

The civil war.

A breathtaking succession of images flashed through his mind, sending it spinning and casting around for the spiritual symbols that had always helped him keep going in life. What he needed to do now was to rearrange that kaleidoscope and to transform it into concrete will-power. When Bakunin[16] had been in prison, he had set himself the daily task of compiling a whole newspaper in his imagination: complete with an editorial and news, short story, serialised story and gossip and miscellaneous columns. The images the music had conjured up had only been a spectacular series of fleeting visions; what he had to do now was to make more permanent sense out of them. The main problem with being held prisoner was preventing oneself at all costs from remaining passive. Perhaps he, Kassner, really could manage to overcome his stupor and his encroaching madness, and his obsession with escape which was tantalising him constantly, keeping him going during his underground existence, just as the prospect of eternal salvation remains a possibility for a Christian, despite his leading a sinful life. But he still had enough strength and will-power left to measure up to the dangers facing him on all sides.

CHAPTER III

The gaily-coloured shop-window of the chandlery that he had seen after his arrest has turned into St Basil's Church, with its multicoloured onion-shaped towers, at the end of the Red Square; and, as if the antique shop's crosses and censers and its entire display of stoles and tunics were levitating, then floating in mid-air, the coppery star-studded domes of a fortified monastery loom into view, adorning the darkness beneath their twofold crosses and gilded ornamental chainwork crowded with pigeons and crows. Below lies a counter-revolutionary city littered with commemorative plaques, trinkets and shrines. This is Old Russia whose blood-steeped blind mysticism barely shrouds the sight of the partisans' corpses that hang from the church bells. The incoming battalion of soldiers from another region, who have been sent as reinforcements up to the stricken partisan army's lines and who are unfamiliar with the area, takes cover in a wood, armed with a single machine-gun. The fortress has dungeons inside it and inside one of these there's a prisoner. He's going to escape. He's in a corridor; behind a frosted-glass window there's a flower, it's barely visible, but there are two splodges of colour, one red, one green, it's all in colour, colour! He's walking towards a plane. His wife's in Prague.[17]

Kassner's mind reeled with escapist fantasies while his body was reeling around his cell. He needed to dredge up every single memory, in minute detail, that was it, then he had to reassemble each one, meticulously. Mustn't let oneself get carried away: one had to build anew, that's what. Not that he was particularly enamoured of his past life, he had pinned his hopes on the future too much for that, but now, having found a real aim, his disjointed memory had regained its powers. Patiently, and with dogged determination, he turned his thoughts back to the wood, with its anxious occupants, opposite the town which nestled inside its foggy hollow.

Darkness hugs the wintry ground, leaden with an oppressive presence which slowly invades the entire nocturnal landscape: processions inch their way slowly across it, appearing then disappearing from view behind a rocky escarpment, the moonlight glimmering on the false pearls of the Russian banners and Orthodox crosses being wielded aloft like cudgels as they file along. A wild boar trundles past, rustling through the leaves: one of the partisans is escaping, his mouth gaping wide open and his blank-looking eyes reflecting the glaucous moonlight; an Orthodox priest in full regalia appears on the hillock, clinging to one of the banners' poles he has used to hoist himself up, letting it take his full weight, the material slapping wildly in the wind that has just got up.

Kassner waits for the slapping sound to reach him. Nothing. No sound whatever — just complete and utter silence. No rustling in the leaves either, none of the sleeping world's usual nocturnal murmurings; no sound of a wild boar cantering off like his neighbour had made earlier on, and that wide-open mouth is screaming — and he can't hear anything.

Deaf! He could hear his scream echoing to the very core of his brain; plus the noise of the grille the guard had just opened. The latter contemplated the prisoner standing there blinded by the light and gasping in anguish, panting as heavily as if he were wearing a stifling cowl, shrugged his shoulders and slammed the grille shut again with such a deafening din it sent Kassner plunging back down into the depths of his controlled madness, entombing him once more.

The priests, who've emerged from behind the hillock by now, begin to move on, their robes and mitres clearly visible beneath the crosses and banners, the whole scene looking infinitely unreal as this goldsmith's folly, this marching treasure-trove[18] spills out across the muddy fields with all its ghostly white beards and pearls and silver glinting in the moonlight. They draw nearer, chanting; it sounds more like an indignant hate-filled drone, they're singing the very chorus that's been lurking around the cell for hours and which modulates into a rustling of leaves, like the sound of floundering, fleeing animals and finally lapses into a distant clanking of silver armour. Something else carries through the darkness: a dog howling in the distance, yet it's as present as the shadow of a bird, hovering closely, wings outstretched.

No: it's a prisoner howling in a nearby cell.

Kassner concentrates with all his might, watching a tiny animal, either a rat or a ferret, scurry away and bolt towards the priests who've now come to a standstill, dwarfed by the vast lunar landscape. Even though their crosses look more like clubs they're unarmed and it's hard to shoot at a defenceless man when he's not running for cover; they're fiddling with some tiny objects from which smoke is rising, immediately turning into clouds of dust which look like they're hanging in the moonlight, seemingly frozen in mid-flight despite the wind: they're incense-burners.

How long is it since he last smoked a cigarette?... The night air wafts the odour of churches towards Kassner, the smell seems intrusive as it steals stealthily over the long line of supplicants standing motionless out there in the countryside beneath the sparkling star-studded heavens, frozen solid with cold and hatred; while the pungent odour of crypts gradually takes hold, stronger even than the bitter box-wood smell of the leaves. Another line suddenly emerges from behind the hillock, bristling with row upon row of menacing crosses. Behind them troop the Whites who, thanks to them, had retaken the village yesterday — and, for more than an hour now, the sound of a tortured peasant, a Red, screaming, has been echoing through the dreary sunlight of a winter's afternoon...

It's the prisoner in the next cell screaming again. A man's imagination can dream up all kinds of torture — Kassner plasters his hands over his ears.

A shot rings out from behind the crosses: one of the Whites is firing. Almost immediately another shot rings out, this time one of the priests is firing (has he got a revolver?); a third one, coming from the woods, makes a red glow there, just like the censers did. Now the recently-arrived battalion's machine-gun starts firing — from slightly to Kassner's rear. Prudently, he moves back. Its steady rat-a-tat sounds like a key being rattled along the bars of a prison cell; the tip of a branch drops down, torn off by a stray bullet and is blown sideways by the wind. Kassner had manned this very same machine-gun when he'd been in the Caucasus; when he'd had to cool down the gun's barrel by holding fistfuls of squashed grapes above it, letting the juice dribble down on to it where it made a "hissing" sound as it boiled upon contact with the metal. A priest is felled, the third one that night; he goes down grabbing frantically at his cross, as if he were twirling round it; the others start running, only to find themselves in the midst of the Whites who capture them straightaway. The machine-gun quickens its tempo while the ancient rifles begin firing from the woods, their shots flickering here and there in short-lived bursts of flame: the partisans have finally seen the Whites — yet all those fatally-wounded bodies plunging to the ground look pathetically insignificant in the vast, indifferent silence of that starlit scene.

"Where are you from?" the machine-gunner asks Kassner.

"I'm a Communist, from abroad."

Silence having fallen once more, there's just the wind, and the black night.

"I'm from the Altai[19] myself. Look at them lying on the ground, with their silvery robes and long white beards: why do they look just like those pockets of unmelted snow that hang around in crevices in the mountains?..."

The dead bodies lying spreadeagled on the night-blackened ground had formed the shape of a giant white vulture with torn-off wings as they had fallen.

Inside the cell, a low but distinctly clear voice whispers solemnly: "They're dead." Then, slightly louder: "Anna's dead too, I tell you... She's dead." Kassner felt his blood throbbing beneath his hands that were still pinned against his ears; it was dredging up memories like a diver sucks in air; while, bubbling vigourously underwater, then repeatedly threshing and flailing the earth and coursing steadily through the dead of night, the blood, his blood, remained his sole, living companion. The walls of his cell were beginning to close in upon Kassner; no, it was the surging tide of his own anguish which was ebbing and flowing with every throb of his buzzing temples. Get back to the town, back to the town!

Is that phantom-ship, scudding along with the desolate clouds that look like bell-buoys adrift in the heavens, miles away from its dead crew whose corpses, still in full uniform, lie strewn across the frozen plains; is that ship actually the same monastery, or not? Why watch with such fascination, so complacently, as a bearded bloke — in a gold-brocade doublet, and standing at the foot of the wall the dead partisans' bodies are still dangling over because they're still hanging from the enormous black bells that the crows are ringing with their non-stop pecking — raises his arm and uses his vodka-filled glass to catch a couple of snowflakes in mid-air as they gently float down? There he stands in the profoundly dense, brooding silence, surrounded by hundreds of pieces of gilt furniture which have transformed the main street into a weird-looking drawing-room, which looks disturbingly cosy beneath the lowering sky and increasingly yellow-tinged clouds. Captured at dawn by a swirling whirlwind of men and frozen leaves amid the last tattered remnants of the night, the town's most affluent houses have had all their over-elaborate furniture, anything that Russian baroque fashion could have possibly concocted from a combination of Louis XV and "Escargot"[20] styles, dragged out by the partisans; there's a giant bouquet of artificial white flowers standing on the largest piano which has feet shaped like cathedrals' gargoyles. It looks just as if there's a carnival going on inside: a throng of bearded partisans is parading around, having stripped the priests of their chasubles and, in the space of a few hours, they've hacked them about and refashioned the old brocade garments into garb that looks like costumes out of the Tales of Hoffmann.[21] Like a bunch of madmen who have suddenly rushed on-stage and taken over the performance at an Opera House, they saunter between the silvered and gilded armchairs and pianos in the murky light, just as the snow is starting to fall. A distant, rumbling sound rises disquietingly from the ground but is muffled by the snow...

Holding out against the powerful tide of images, Kassner continued to monitor the dull pounding noise as it came nearer, and heard the urgent trampling sound turning into the more regular puffing of a steamship. Abandoning both the armchairs and their fantasies, the partisans ran back into the houses... A few shots rang out, then — nothing: the fighting had stopped. Nothing whatsoever remained of anything at all except for the blood pounding and pulsating in his temples, then rasping at the very bowels of the earth, sounding even louder as it was mingling with a furious whinnying: the cavalry had arrived.

Look at the corner! Thousands of riderless horses were galloping into the town, still saddled and harnessed in all their semi-Oriental finery. They raced in with the loose, irresolute stride of animals that have reverted to the wild, swerving sharply to gallop into the main street, veering erratically, like the flapping sails of a ship blown off-course by the wind, as they bolted through, sending divans and armchairs flying in a frenzied tumult of hooves and whinnying. On they raced, their necks jerking violently up and down in front of their heaving foam-flecked backs, hemmed in by the confines of the street like bulls piling through the gate of a corral, their ceremonial apparel making them look like ghostly apparitions resurrected from prehistoric migrations. The last of the partisans were fleeing before them, dwarfed by the immense, turbulent torrent that was flooding the road from end to end like a tidal wave with a sea of bobbing and heaving, galloping bodies, under the watchful but unseeing eyes of the dirty tick-ridden horses which were twitching nervously behind the wooden fences: the fleeing Cossacks[22] had abandoned their own beasts. The partisans stood watching enviously, coveting the wasted potential for abundant riches as it sped past in a seemingly endless supply — until, eventually, they saw the peasants' horses appear, bringing up the rear behind the Cossacks' animals. They had broken down the fences as the others had galloped past and, saddleless and barebacked, looking as naked as nude human bodies compared with the others' ornate harnesses they, too, bolted in turn.

The clattering racket the cantering clusters of horses' hooves were making synchronised into a single sound as, with total abandon, they galloped off recklessly into the gathering twilight, fanning out gradually as they raced towards the woods, already shrouded in semi-darkness. Despite the grief and war that lurked in hiding somewhere beyond the mountains, they were living symbols of the world's thrilling vibrancy and joyful outburst of exuberance as it exulted in the invigorating icy air. Air! Icy, cold intangible air, nothing like solid prison walls, freezing cold air which reared up at you like one of those horses, the last of which, wildly tossing their heads, were fast disappearing — rearing up out of the icy darkness and stamping on the open, cracked ground, on the earth that was as full of life as the flowing rivers and seas are, trampling it brutally with barbaric hooves!

Kassner opened his eyes again.

Nothing to cut or harm oneself with. Not a rope, nor even a handkerchief. Could he use his nails to cut his veins open? He realised that they were not long enough yet.

Couldn't he find something else? A friend of his had asked for one of his veins to be severed after his death so that he could be sure his circulation really would have stopped. Kassner distinctly remembered the sight of the scalpel an assistant was using (the doctor had refused to do it) to poke around in the flesh which by then had stopped bleeding, searching for the thin, white vein. He'd poke around for his own in the same way, even if he couldn't see it, he'd try to find his own plump, pulsating vein, getting his fingertips all bloody while he fumbled for it...

His body which had seemed so vulnerable earlier on now felt fully alive, with his heart and lungs protected by his bony ribcage, it felt mutely, indomitably alive. "Nature organises things as if men were always wanting to commit suicide..."

He just wanted to die in peace but at the same time felt an urge to sink his thumbs into the neck of the first guard to come in next and not let go, whatever happened afterwards... How on earth could one make one's own death be of use to someone else? It was utterly impossible to help anyone else from inside this hole. "To have had so many opportunities of dying..." Fate didn't select people very well or give them much choice. He'd have to go back to trying to use his nails.

It wouldn't be all that simple. He walked over to the strip of light that was filtering in around the door-frame and just managed to make out the vague shape of his hand with its outstretched fingers; unable to see his nails he guessed that they were very short. He would use his little fingernail like a vaccination blade. He tried to cut into the skin near his wrist with it. Useless. It wasn't only too short, it was also too round and blunt: his skin was tougher and more elastic than he'd thought. He'd have to sharpen his nail by rubbing it against the wall to file it down to a point. At least another two more days to go.

He was still trying to see his fingers properly but could only vaguely make out his fingertips which loomed indistinctly out of the darkness as if they belonged to someone else's hand. His courage began to mutate into a deadly implacability. Fascinated by that almost invisible bit of what was incredibly his very own skin, where the nail which would help him kill himself was going to grow slowly but surely, he glued his eyes to it, spellbound.

He began to walk around again. His hand, that hand which was going to become his fatal weapon, dangled down at his side like a tool-bag. The coming hour would be exactly the same as this one; the thousands of muffled little noises filling the silence of the prison would carry on sounding like swarms of over-burdened bugs teeming endlessly around, living out their exhausting existence until the end of time, and a layer of equally anguished suffering would envelop that never-changing realm of nothingness, like a stifling blanket of dust.

He leant against the wall and went back to contemplating the stagnant passage of time.

CHAPTER IV

The light was coming from a lamp at the end of the corridor. It was probably dark outside.

The guard was looking at him consideringly, standing there with his feet planted wide apart. This bloke feels like having a bit of fun, thought Kassner. He'd heard about prisoners being made to crawl around on all fours.

The guard took a step forward.

Kassner was convinced he was facing either cruelty personified or someone's compulsive urge to inflict humiliation on another, yet the face confronting him looked scarcely more menacing than a slave trader's. He stepped backwards to keep his distance, tilting his trunk slightly forwards and lifting his left heel: if he speaks to me, I shan't say anything, but if he tries to touch me, I'll head-butt him in the stomach. We'll see what happens afterwards.

The guard was not fooled: someone who is recoiling in fear tilts his torso backwards, not forwards. Something fell on to the floor with a thud.

"Here's some work. Unravel it," he said.

The door closed again.

When Kassner had been feeling closest to committing suicide, just facing reality had been enough to revive him and make him regain his strength. Earlier, even when the SA men had come into his cell, and in spite of the screams coming from the cells nearby, his fears and distress had evaporated the minute they had come in. He well knew what suffering from insomnia was like, with its tendency to make one keep going over and over one's problems and sorrows in every minute detail with insect-like precision: that was the sort of world he was struggling in. If he was going to win the battle it wasn't going to be by achieving any peace of mind, that was obviously out of the question, it would be by keeping his head poised and clenched fists drawn, ready to strike. Besides, he had so completely lost his sense of touch he would have lashed out as uncontrollably as a starving person grabbing food and cramming it into his mouth.

He stepped on the object the guard had thrown on the floor and picked it up: it was a rope.

Surely one could eat a rope if it was nicely grilled? Oh, for a purple-tinged slice of roast meat, beads of water condensing on the sides of some cool, misted carafes of water, chilled aniseed and peppermint cordials in the evenings, drunk in the shade of trees! How many times had he been given something to eat since he'd been in here? Hunger was making him feel as dazed and feverish as one gets during a nasty bout of flu, but only every now and then.

"Work..."

It occurred to him that unravelling the rope would whittle down his nails; suicide had come back in person looking for him like a lost object, it seemed. The metallic clunking of doors being slammed shut, one by one, rose in an ascending scale of sounds breaking the deep, pitch-black silence: the guards were obviously handing out some more ropes. Had thoughts of suicide chosen this very moment to enter into each prison-hole, along with each of the ropes, biding their time, like despair bides its time and mental exhaustion bides its time, waiting for the right moment to strike? Were the waves of madness that had drowned then abandoned Kassner earlier on now sweeping up his comrades in their swirling currents, sucking them further and further down into the depths and carrying them further and further distant from their real, former selves? Weren't they grabbing the rope, that Nazi rope being dangled in front of them; weren't they being driven mad by the thought that the only gesture they could make to prove they were still free men had been foreseen and that, just as their lives had been snatched away from them, now their death too, was being snatched out of their control?... Some of those men had been in their cells much longer than he had and what about the younger ones and the men who were ill... There was a rope now in every one of those dungeons and all Kassner could do was knock on the wall.

Knock after knock. He hardly dared to listen. Yet, either he'd gone completely mad already, or someone was answering. From the same direction as the last time. Even while he was straining with all his might to listen for it, he was terrified of hearing it: the knocking might stop again, mightn't it? He'd thought he'd heard the guard coming along once already, but had been mistaken. Hope itself had become a source of pain.

Patiently, with that infinite, inexhaustible patience that only prisoners have, the invisible hand started again:

Five - two - two, six - nine - ten - one, four - one, four - two, six - nine.

There was a longer pause between nine and ten than between two and six.

When Kassner had been knocking on the wall, he had not tried working out an alphabet-based code. It didn't matter, the main thing was that communication had been established: by just listening, and not even giving any answering knocks, he was doing as much to rescue his comrade from the empty depths of despair as he was to rescue himself from equal torment. The grouping of the numbers in twos: two-six, one-four, was obviously not based on a system which divided the alphabet into assigned numbers since each group was followed by individual numerical figures. This meant that they were almost certainly arithmetical numbers. 5-2-26-9-10. He'd already forgotten the rest.

He knocked on the wall again, once.

His neighbour answered, once again.

5-2-26; 9-10; 14-14; 26-9.

He began knocking again, at longer intervals, until Kassner had rapped the same numbers in reply.

The latter squeezed his eyelids tightly shut, trying hard to remember the numbers in their correct order, and felt his face scrunching up in a painful grimace, right up to his temples, as he did so. The key to the code was not in the names of the letters but almost certainly in their arithmetical symbols. He felt exactly like a miserly insect storing up its pile of goodies in its hole in a rock, with its legs tucked in — just like his own fingers were clawing at his chest right now — storing up these numbers which were at least symbols of friendship and which either his physical weakness or overworking his mind could wipe from his memory as surely as waking up would.

Even though the numbers seemed to be dangling precariously just behind his eyelids, suspended by an invisible delicate thread, they filled the darkness, hovering above him as if all he had needed to do to save himself was to grab hold of them, but his hand had kept on missing them. He tried out all kinds of different keys for the code: adding assigned figures to the numbers of the letters of the alphabet; subtracting, multiplying and dividing up the alphabet into sections. Just thinking, trying to work out the numbers and escaping from his mental void was such a help that any other obstacle, any other problem would have seemed ludicrously unimportant compared to this. Was it based on an inverted version of the alphabet?... he discovered that he only knew it off by heart one way round, not backwards.

What if the man who was knocking on the wall was insane?

An old anarchist friend of his, who had managed to convert some of his fellow-patients into conscientious objectors when he'd been ill and in a military hospital, had been put in a bed between the wall and a madman in the bed next to him.

There was no reason to suppose that it might not be one of the guards who'd heard his own knocking and was deliberately rapping out a random series of meaningless knocks in reply, was there?

The knocking started again. Only a prisoner would have this kind of patience, a blind man's patience; someone who'd gone off his head could never manage to concentrate so hard and knock on the wall with such painstaking efforts.

If he, himself, could be patient enough, he'd get there! Just so long as his constant rehashing of possible solutions to the coded numbers didn't confuse him totally so that he got them all muddled, ending up completely dazed and desolate, his mind a blank, so near and yet so far from this unflagging display of comradeship...

Besides, all the other noises coming from the prison were beginning to sound like distant knocking and the whole prison-camp began to remind him of the meeting that night in Hamburg when, at his bidding, each of the men there had lit a match and had witnessed the size of the vast crowd of people stretching away into the gloomy distance, punctured with tiny pin-pricks of light before the flames went out, plunging them all into darkness once more... His mind went back to a night when they had been fighting, to a street in the industrial part of the city near the Alexanderplatz with its closed cigar-sellers' shops, all bathed in moonlight. The Communists had just fled the street and, as the rumble of police-vans drew closer and closer, the last lights went out one by one. Then, when the vans had hardly finished going past, rectangles of light — split by jagged silhouettes — began streaming on to the pavements from one end of the road to the other: the street's population had suddenly materialised again, and with strained, tense faces, were standing slightly back from the windows because of the bullets, with the smaller silhouettes of their sneaky little brats beside them. Doors were being opened for any comrades who might have been hiding around corners. Then, all of a sudden, as abruptly as it had materialised, the whole symbolic scene of brotherly feeling and solidarity was lost in darkness once again: another lorry loaded with policemen came along and shot down the street at full speed between the houses which were once more bathed in indifferent moonlight.

Hour after hour went by, with numbers nibbling away at his mind like ants, and with the occasional sound of guards going past. Then, ever so slowly, almost by chance it seemed, as if he had had nothing whatsoever to do with it, the thought occurred to him that 5 might not mean that 1 was the fifth letter, but that the alphabet actually started with the sixth letter. So that meant F equalled 1; G, 2... Z, 21; A, 22; B, 23... E, 26, and so on. The other prisoner began knocking once again and Kassner listened attentively, counting out each knock on his fingers, one by one, and spelling out:

2 = **G**; 26 = **E**; 9 = N.*

He shook with joy, his body once again reacting faster than his mind. Even though he was almost suffocating, he was holding his breath and his fingers had suddenly taken on a mind of their own and were digging into his thighs. Still reeling from it all he suddenly shrank back into the gloom: he could hear a different sound between the knocks; the guard was coming along again.

Slowly. Calm, indifferent even, he was probably riddled with the boredom that was seeping from behind the doors, oozing from the penned-in prisoners' disintegrating minds — he, the guard, was a prisoner of time, amid all those other prisoners who had either sunk into a mouldering stupor or were going to die.

One, two, three, four...

Kassner could obviously hear better, on the inside of his cell, than the guard could from the outside. Five, six... But the guard was getting closer all the time and he would soon be able to hear it. Seven... As the steps came nearer, Kassner felt time transform itself into a seething torrent, rushing towards him like a raging river, tearing away at the remaining shreds of his tattered nerves as he struggled against the current. Eight, nine... If the guard heard anything, not only would the man who was knocking

---

* *Genosse*: comrade. [Author's note.]

be beaten up or sent to the vertical coffins, the tiny cells where a condemned prisoner could only stand upright, but they would find out about the alphabet as well. Kassner felt as fully responsible as if, as a result of his own insensibility and carelessness, the other man who was knocking on the wall with his unceasingly patient endeavours at helping him, and giving him moral support, would give the game away and be lured into a trap. Ten... He was torn between the knocking and the approaching steps which would be on top of him within three seconds... Even if the alphabet really was the one he thought it was, how could he tap out the word *careful,* how could he work out the letters: A, C...?* Starting from F, he counted them out on his fingers. It was more than 20...

He raised his fist, then immediately bent his forefinger, realising that this way he would not be heard...

The other man had just stopped knocking.

Had he, too, heard the guard? Probably: because he, like Kassner, must have been concentrating so hard on listening for the other's knocking, any different noise would surely have caught his attention straightway. Some of the patrols seemed to come round quite regularly. In the now seemingly interminable silence, but with the lingering threat of another signal from the cell next door hanging over him, one after the other the footsteps came nearer. Closely monitoring each step, Kassner lay in wait, shoulders hunched, bracing himself as if to deflect any new signal, coiled like a spring with his frantic efforts at transforming his willpower into some kind of powerful, hypnotic force.

The steps went away.

The knocking began again.

10 = **O**

While the other prisoner was still carrying on, Kassner rapped out:

1, 4 : **S,**   1, 4 : **S;** 2, 6...

Together they rapped out the word: *Comrade,* there in the darkness, certain they could understand each other now, yet neither of them was really interrupting the other one. They carried on to the end without stopping, each one hearing both his own and the other's knocking, just as if, had they been able to, they could have heard their hearts quietly beating in unison.

Kassner just wanted to say the basic essentials, using only the sort of words that would instantly get through to a walled-up prisoner and clutch at his heart-strings. Above all, he wanted to tell the other man that he was not alone, to help him defend himself against the rope that, obviously, he was not unravelling either, since he was knocking

---

* *Achtung*: careful. [Author's note.]

on the wall. Kassner worked out the words he would use, counting them out on his fingers: he had to communicate in a language that he was still having to work out letter by letter; earlier on the other man's accompanying knocks had helped him along. But he could already hear

TAKE HEART

The guard went past.

The other prisoner carried on (and, as Kassner was already rapping out the first couple of letters of WHO, they seemed to be interrupting each other):

WE CAN...

The sound of a door being slammed shut drowned out the knocking. Kassner's ears were hyper-sensitive. He was sure that he could tell where the noises were coming from now and the sound of the slamming door was coming from the same direction as the knocking had earlier.

Either the guards had gone into his friend's cell or they had gone into another one that was near enough for him to have stopped knocking. Something was definitely going on in there; a smothered kind of sound, both too far-off and indistinct for him to make out what it was and which was rather like the muffled echoes distant sounds make when they travel through water; something set every one of his already strained senses tingling, fraught as he was in that pitch-dark gloom. There it came again, another knock! No it wasn't: that was a thump. It was followed by another more muffled, but more substantial thud. The thumping was becoming more and more frequent, sounding louder and heavier now: it wasn't just his finger any longer, it was the whole of his friend's body being battered and flung around his cell, and it was either the soft thudding of his flesh or the clearer, sharper sound of his head hitting the wall which was echoing around Kassner. He stood there in his own cell, cooped up in the gloom, wide-eyed and gaping, beside himself with helplessness and his sense of utter, abject powerlessness. He waited for them to come in.

Maybe they wouldn't though. They had most probably only heard the knocking coming from the one side (he, himself, had been knocking far less frequently); otherwise, they would have waited to see who was answering, and now...

They did not come in, however. It was solitude, loneliness, in fact, that was going to come back. Cut off from friendship now, just as earlier he had been drained of dreams and devoid of hope, Kassner was left stranded and straining his ears in the silence which spread like a blanket over those hundreds of other keyed-up minds and pent-up wills in that black termite's nest. If he could only speak on behalf of those men, even if they could never hear him!

"Comrades, all of you around me here in the darkness..."

However many hours, however many days it took him, he'd spend them preparing something he could say out loud, into that gloomy darkness...

CHAPTER V

"Ever since... I'm no longer sure: time loses all meaning in the dark — anyway, a fortnight before I was arrested — I was in Paris: at a rally for the prisoners in Germany. There were tens of thousands of our people packed in there, it was standing room only. In the main hall, the blind men standing in the front rows specially reserved for them were singing softly — their voices drowned out by the rousing revolutionary songs which were echoing around the other rooms and outside into the darkness — and making those pitiful gestures blind people do when they sing. They were singing for us. Because we are in here.

"After he'd died, I saw Lenin's corpse, in the old "Hall of Nobility".[23] His skull seemed even larger than usual, would you believe. And the queues of people went on trudging through the snow until well into the night.

"After we'd filed in front of the coffin — or maybe it was before — we waited in a nearby house. When Lenin's wife arrived, looking like an elderly schoolmistress as usual, we realised that the deepest silence can become even more profound than before. People were waiting expectantly. Everyone was extremely distressed. And she became aware that we all understood and were giving her moral support in the very presence of death itself.

"And then, in that tone of voice one uses on that kind of occasion, d'you see, she said, very simply — and none of us present imagined that that seasoned Communist woman would ever say such a thing: 'Comrades, Vladimir Ilyich deeply loved ordinary people...'

"You, my companions who were buried alive out in China,[24] my friends who had their eyes gouged out in Russia, my friends locked in with your ropes around me here in Germany, you my friend, whom they've probably just beaten senseless, it's what we all have in common and which binds us together that I call love."

"I know how much effort and will-power it takes to bring about a just and meaningful outcome. I know too that nothing will ever compensate us for the amount of suffering so many of us here are going through, except victory in our struggle. But at least, if we are victorious, every one of our people will eventually manage to have a proper life. And so will all those men who know they are alone, who know they will go home to an empty, lonely room at night, and know they will be carrying the burden of people's contempt and indifference, and the pointlessness of their lives, which shadow them everywhere dogging their heels, back in there with them. And they know they will then go and look for a woman, any woman, to live with, because one has to have someone to live with; and they'll sleep together and will have children, at random with no thought for their future, just brats, before eventually going to seed themselves and rotting away among the masses of other infertile seeds which will never have germinated. At this very moment, wherever it's dark outside like it is in here, there are masses of hunted, haunted people silently sitting down or going to bed in every house. Because really loving someone means making a choice, and one can't make a choice when one has nothing to give.

"But, at this very minute, from the blind men in Paris to the Chinese Soviets, in every country throughout the world, there are men thinking of us, men who care about us as if we were their own dead children.

"I have seen...

"I'll have to think back... It's difficult to speak in the dark...

"My father was one of the best militant campaigners they had at Gelsenkirchen for over twenty years. Then my mother died and he began drinking heavily. He used to stagger along to meetings at night, blind drunk, rather like people who've once narrowly escaped starving to death and get up at night and lurch around looking for the bread they've hidden under their pillows. He would interrupt the speakers, fool around or sometimes just sit quietly at the back of the hall. They all knew him and they would see him arrive and watch him sadly, or with exasperation, but they would never eject him. 'He's a welcome distraction,' I heard a comrade, who had not seen me behind him, say ironically one day... It was my father who'd given me my political training — before all that. When I was making my first speeches he tried giving up alcohol, but always relapsed. I found it hard to stomach his constant interruptions speech after speech, but I took it on the chin and it was then that I understood how very committed I was to the revolution. He worked down the mines. One day there was an explosion: he was below ground with two hundred other miners. Comrades from the emergency rescue service went down there, while the funeral bell tolled unbearably on and on. The flames had hemmed them in and, although they had been wearing their masks, they had been unable to save even their own men: two were killed, one was missing. The volunteers — every one of us, you can imagine — who were standing by the pit's shaft-head formed a chain and passed along extinguishers and sandbags while an ambulance, making the only audible sound there, stood by waiting, in vain. The fire spread — and a third rescuer was killed. It went on like that for forty hours. Then the inspection team's surveyors and our own delegates eventually announced that all the tunnels had filled up with carbon monoxide, and the mine was slowly and methodically blocked up in front of our eyes...

"I saw a play in Moscow, which was about a very similar event, on the day of the Youth Festival. Three hundred thousand young people were marching on parade. We had to cut through their ranks to get into the theatre: the performance started at nine o'clock and the parade had started at five. Every time there was an interval we went downstairs to have a cigarette, and each time we did so we saw that unending youthful procession, bristling with red flags held aloft bobbing along at window level, still going past. Then we all went upstairs again, the other spectators returning to what was dramatic fiction for them, whereas I was returning to scenes from my youth. And at every interval we went downstairs again and, yet again, we saw all those young people still going past, and then we went back upstairs yet again, to that play which had been seen and heard as far away as the Caspian Sea and even the Pacific, because it expressed the dignity and meaning of people's toil and struggles. I remembered that tolling bell and the miners huddled round, isolated, amid the general lack of concern which extended into the very depths of the indifferent German night... And when the play was over and I was looking at the crowds milling around, preventing us from leaving the theatre straightaway, it struck me that these people were all under twenty years old. So none of those young men who had been converging on the Red Square for the last few hours, not a single one of them, d'you see, had ever known that time of brutal oppression...

"We..."

A couple of footsteps sounded out in the corridor.

Without knowing why, Kassner moved towards the door.

"We are all in there together, in that walled-up mine. And our newspapers, which did not have any correspondents in the factories at the time now do, ever since anyone writing in to us has run the risk of ending up in this dungeon. But in spite of the fact that these dens of insanity really do exist, five million people still voted "no" during the plebiscite.[25]

"You see..."

The door opened and the blindingly harsh light from the corridor bored through his eyes making his very brain feel on fire. It streamed over his entire body, washing away the clinging, gloomy darkness which had been gluing his eyelids together.

"Are you going to make your mind up, then?"

He finally managed to open his eyes. Two red and green men were standing there, dotted with bright yellow spots which dazzled him... They turned khaki-coloured... SA uniforms with the black swastikas on their white arm-bands; white, an unbearably disturbing colour... Kassner felt himself being pushed outside.

They took him off through great swathes of yellow light which flooded around them as they went. They knew he was Kassner by now. Could he try to escape? He could barely control his movements any longer; he wouldn't be able to grab anyone or struggle at all... Besides he could hardly see properly. "I'll become human again, once they start torturing me." With his recent speech still fluttering around in his mind like the damaged wings of a wounded bird, he drifted along like a child's balloon, buoyed up by the tang of the sweeter-smelling air now filling his lungs, by the great strides they were making, and by the light which had now turned blue as it does when one takes off a pair of dark glasses: here came the ground floor, daylight. "In an hour's time maybe, I should just about be able to flatten one of them, in spite of everything."

It was only when he found himself facing a Nazi official in the very same room where they had interrogated him when he had arrived at the camp, that he realised they were not taking him to either the main guard-room or the basement, not yet. Was he going to be transferred to another camp? Apart from the pitch-black cells there were only vertical coffins here. Because of the dust-filled daylight streaming down upon the man's face, Kassner could only make out that he had a thick but well-trimmed moustache and bushy eyebrows, and that there were also two shadowy figures there in plain clothes, leaning against the wall looking just like a couple of hanging overcoats. A shaft of dust-speckled sunlight shimmered in front of them like a wind-swept canal. Kassner signed a register, the Nazi handed over an envelope and a battered paper-wrapped parcel with holes in it, through which the prisoner thought he could see his braces, to one of the two overcoats. One of them opened it:

"There's a lighter and a box of cachou sweets missing."

"They're wrapped up in the handkerchief," the Nazi replied.

The two men took the stumbling prisoner to a car: he could not stop looking up at the sky, and caught his foot on every obstacle, tripping himself up, then completely missed the pavement. They got in and sat down, one on each side of him, and the car drove off immediately.

"At last!" said the first overcoat.

Even though it was extremely likely that his companions were members of the Gestapo, Kassner felt like making some sort of savage remark in reply. The bulky man who had just been speaking looked faintly unreal out there in the clean, blue-washed open air, with his droopy, wispy moustache straggling down over his barely concealed canine teeth and each of his pronounced, heavy features somehow distorting his face into a virtual caricature of himself. He looked to Kassner like both the walrus and its fat, Chinese owner who had put it on display, he had once seen in Shanghai. Although Kassner was conscious of his mania for instantly seeing a resemblance to some animal or other in every face he saw, this particular face was inordinately peculiar. Moreover, this face, which was being periodically galvanised into life by the constant flashing of the slanting light pouring in through the car's windows, was quivering queerly above its owner's fingers with their rounded, strangely curved nails. It was becoming blurred with the relentless flickering, as though it were about to vanish into the shimmering light. Everything was being thrown backwards in the car, but the policemen's faces too had turned into restless and vulnerable, transitory images, ready to melt away into the dappled, iridescent air. He was not dreaming: every object there actually existed, was its proper size and weighed what it normally weighed; but did not seem real at all. This was a different planet, an alien world, they had reached the shadowy domain of the unknown.

"So, we're going to see the old girl then, are we?" enquired the walrus.

What "old girl", Kassner wondered. Even so, he willed himself not to ask where they were taking him.

The walrus smiled silently, or was it ironically, his canine teeth clearly visible now against a blurred background of autumnal fields and trees. Kassner had the impression that it was the canines talking to him, not the mouth.

"You're obviously feeling better now," said the walrus.

Kassner was humming — the Orthodox priests' droning chant, but he was humming it more rhythmically and cheerfully — then he eventually realised what he was doing. He felt free again: only his mind still felt threatened. Maybe the walrus was going to dissolve, maybe the car would disappear and he would find himself back inside his dungeon. Maybe what he was hearing and seeing had no connection with anything or anyone, and all thoughts, ideas and words had merged together, escaping into thin air, into nothingness, along with the mauve asters and the trees which were whizzing past on either side of the road. Yet, while a part of him remained lucidly aware and on the watch, all about him, whether it was reality, dream or death, a vast imaginary world calling itself earth whirled past at full tilt.

"All the same," the walrus went on, nodding his head, "you're lucky that he decided to give himself up."

"Who?"

"Kassner."

In exactly the same way as when a pair of binoculars are slowly adjusted and an image gradually comes into focus, the policeman's face crystallised and stood out against the bright light. Kassner's mind flashed back to the sight of two Red Guards lying on the ground at the entrance to a village, one Siberian morning filled with the happy sound of buzzing insects; they were dead, both of them, their genitals burnt between a couple of bricks.

"Have they got proof it's him?"

"He's confessed."

Silence.

"People confess to plenty of things here," said Kassner.

"You haven't been ill-treated at all. The swine hadn't even been beaten up. If he had been, fair enough. But anyway, in a word, he confessed of his own free will."

The policeman with the pale eyebrows frowned.

"Everyone knew we were looking for him — and that we'd have done whatever it took to get him. In a word, whatever it took. We'd already begun. But he gave himself up."

"Whatever it took... Suppose he was the kind of bloke who'd wanted to spare the others all that?"

"You're joking of course? A Communist! I don't think he ever really knew what other people's punishment was like. It was only when he knew that it was actually him we were looking for that he gave himself up. In a word, you're going barmy because you're in a blue funk about coming back here..."

Had he finally gone off his head? This dream-like grey sky with its angry, lowering clouds, this man who looked like a walrus, this flickering world which seemed about to dissolve at any minute, and more, this windscreen he could not even recognise his own hairy face in; all this at the very moment he was being obliged to talk about himself as if he were someone else...

"There are some photos of him, I think. Anyway, he knew the risks he was taking," resumed the walrus.

"Where is he?"

The policeman shrugged his shoulders.

"Dead?"

"I'd be surprised if he were still in one piece. I'm amazed they ever believed you were an important member of the Communist party, when you ask daft questions like that. In a word, he was a swine, but he wasn't a complete idiot."

The car drove past a railway station. Some prisoners were working on the track. Standing by a train that was about to leave, a man who was obviously going to travel on it and a woman were kissing, watched by most of the prisoners.

"He wasn't a swine."

"If you'd been hurt instead of him, would you have thought he was such a decent chap?"

Kassner was looking at the man and woman who were still kissing.

"If I... Yes."

The other policeman laid his hand on Kassner's arm:

"If you really insist on going back..."

But the walrus quickly tapped his head with his finger.

That man either turned himself in to save other people from being tortured, thought Kassner, or because he wanted to kill himself; or maybe he was hoping to get a comrade freed he thought might be more useful than he was: me... When people are really off their heads, can they really be convinced they're not mad? Some man had probably died instead of him; he knew it, was thinking about it, yet could not bring himself mentally to fully register the fact; he felt as agonised as if someone had been trying to break his will by torturing his child. Even while he was asking himself these questions, he was still obsessed by thoughts of his dungeon, unable to tear his mind away from it.

"Don't you have a photo of him?"

The policeman shrugged his shoulders and waved his hand indifferently.

Maybe he wasn't mad and it was all a pack of lies?

Maybe the walrus was making it all up, to force him into saying something. Or just doing all this for pure pleasure? Ever since Kassner had left the prison-camp he had not felt he was truly in the real world, not for a single second. But was he still capable of telling what was reality and what wasn't?

"If you hadn't been in contact with people a foreigner who respected the host-country's hospitality shouldn't have met, nothing would have happened to you," said the other policeman, "you're really lucky your legation took up your case and is looking after you. They've got it all wrong, mind you!"

True, his own people were bound to be on friendly terms with some of the members of the Czechoslovakian legation.

Kassner's eyes were finally getting used to daylight again: he looked at the man who had just been speaking. Conventionally middle-class and stockily built, with a face that was a perfect example of a policeman's "mug". Yet, even though Kassner's eyesight was almost back to normal, his mind still remained stubbornly tied to his dungeon by a thousand cobwebs. Did the walrus believe he'd said too much? He'd turned away and was contemplating the fields which were being strafed by swirling eddies of leaves.

... Until they reached the Polizei-Präsidium, (Police H.Q.) where, after various statements and formalities had been gone through, a clerk with a bad cold handed Kassner back his parcel (braces and shoelaces inside) and the German marks that had been confiscated from him:

"I'm keeping back 11.70 marks."

"For stamps?"

"No, for the camp. It's 1.30 marks per day."

"That's not much. Have I only been here nine days?"

Kassner had begun reconciling himself to the real world by now, but the idea that he had been in his dungeon for only nine days made him feel totally disconnected from it once more; reality seemed like a language he had once learnt then forgotten again. The shattering thought occurred to him that his wife had been incredibly lucky, as if she had been set free and he had not.

"There are two for you to go towards your journey home from Germany. Unless between now and then..."

"What do you mean, between now and then?"

The man with the cold did not reply. Anyway, there was no point: Kassner knew that he would never be safe until he had crossed the border. How had the Nazis managed to fall for the identity of the man who had turned himself in for his sake? They were guaranteed a corpse anyway, maybe they had some obscure, powerful motives for their action that he would never find out. Whoever he might have been, had they killed him before the documents arrived at the camp where Kassner had been imprisoned? If it was Wolf, he could easily have got hold of papers bearing Kassner's name, but he looked nothing like him...

Kassner contemplated the heavy skies and lowering clouds above the rooftops: civilian aircraft had probably been unable to leave the aerodrome. He had to take advantage of being expelled from Germany, he had to leave the country as soon as possible so that he could change his identity: he and the Gestapo would meet again, quite soon. His gaze travelled down the buildings, storey by storey. A man had probably died for him. In the street below, everyday life was carrying on as normal.

Would the factory's plane be able to take off?

CHAPTER VI

When he had seen the anonymous man he was to fly somewhere, the pilot had thought he recognised Kassner, but had not asked him any questions. The small propeller factory owned by the Party's underground organisation permitted him to carry out a few test flights every week plus the use of two planes. This one would return in a month's time, bearing a different number and flown by a different pilot. Kassner tore his gaze away from the wonderfully pink ham inside the sandwich he was holding, and picked up the weather information sheet giving the day's meteorological conditions: visibility becoming poor 10 kilometres from the airfield; hailstorms over the Bohemian mountains, low cloud cover, foggy conditions at ground level in many areas.

"Pretty bad, eh?" said the pilot.

Kassner looked at the smile which lit up the nervy, sparrow-like face despite the prospect of such a departure (is it true that pilots always look like birds?):

"I was a look-out during the war, you know. Have the airliners taken off?"

"No. Permission's refused for take-off towards the South from the airfield."

"Refused for German planes; what about Czech planes?"

"They haven't been able to leave either. They've only a one in three chance of going."

Thoughtfully, Kassner looked again at this man he knew nothing about, except for his passionate commitment to the cause, yet with whom he was going to risk his own life. Friendship was extremely important to him; but the fact that, although they were not linked by any personal ties, their commitment to what they both cared about so passionately bound them to one another almost as intimately, moved him even more deeply. It was as if each step they took towards the aircraft was carrying him closer and closer to a Spartan-like, but still profound friendship, so very rare in this world.

"Let's chance it," said Kassner, "I'd rather crash on the other side of the border."

"Right."

They continued walking towards the machine, which was lying, lifeless, on the airfield and — so awfully tiny and flimsy looking, flimsy, flimsy...

"We'll take off northwards," said the pilot, "in weather like this we'll be out of sight in ten minutes."

They reached their plane and stood beside it: only a small amount of spare fuel, and only one single engine. Obviously a light aircraft for weekend flights.

"Does it have a transmitter?"[26] asked Kassner.

"No."

It didn't really matter that much to him anyway.

Passports and documents were stamped for the last time and parachutes clipped into place.

"Ready. Ignition on?"

"Ignition on."

Throttle open.

The plane gained height. Although Kassner could not see any trees moving, the headwind was alternately lifting the plane then dropping it, tossing it to and fro and making it pitch continuously in slow motion like a warship at sea. Below, beneath some patches of cloud there were flocks of birds (flying very low and skimming so close to the ground they looked as if they were glued to it, grounded like human beings). A lone train was chugging along through the empty autumnal landscape in the intense, calm afternoon light, its ribbon of smoke streaming out far and wide behind it, like an urban smog hanging in the air above the sleepy villages scattered about like herds of placid animals. Soon there was nothing left beneath the heavy skies but the flights of birds hugging the ground like shoals of fish skimming the peaceful sandbanks of a deep watery grave; hamlets, woods and vegetation seemed to be gradually fusing together and merging into a single, calmer and more peaceful existence, well beyond the world of prison-camps. Yet there was almost certainly a concentration camp somewhere out there in that very same landscape where, with the tireless, persistent cruelty of children, men were torturing other men, inflicting such agony upon them they ended up losing all hope. The memory of that black gloom broke into his reverie, diverting both his mind and his gaze from the contemplation of that vast, biblical panorama, weighing down his spirits and blanking out all thoughts save those still preoccupied with cruelty and suffering as if, like the woods and open plains, they were the only things to have survived the passing of so many thousands of years. But, right there in front of him, the pilot's face stood out against that backdrop of plains and clouds; he was concentrating hard. What they were doing together bound them to one another like a solid, enduring friendship. The pilot was there, a substantial fixture silhouetted against an increasingly whiter background, as blankly innocent as the replies of those men Kassner had saved by erasing their names from lists; as blank as those of the shadowy, anonymous crowd he had addressed in his speech, and the silent host of its members which had peopled the black gloom in the prison now seemed to be filling the foggy universe around him: the vast grey world inhabited solely by this willing, valiant little machine which was even more highly strung than a wild animal.

The plane's altitude had increased from one to two thousand metres; it flew into a dense bank of fog. Despite being absorbed in his reverie, a part of Kassner's mind still remained on the alert, constantly listening to the engine and on the lookout for the first gap in the clouds through which he'd be able to catch another fleeting glimpse of the ground below. He'd only been able to find an inaccurately-scaled map in the cabin, and the clouds were so thick it was impossible to observe the lie of the land and take any bearings. All sense of time evaporated while this peculiar, dream-like struggle went on in the midst of the now uniformly unbroken bank of fog. Once they emerged from it, would it be Germany he saw, or Czechoslovakia or one of those Asiatic landscapes he'd flown over so often, dotted with Imperial ruins buzzing with wasps, and mules, ears askew, trudging along in the poppy-filled wind?... Compasses don't indicate a plane's drift when the wind is blowing at rightangles. As they emerged from this prolonged, laborious grind through the dense expanse of fog, a ridge of snow-capped, jagged mountain peaks suddenly loomed straight ahead against the darkening cloud-filled sky, at the very point where the map only showed low hills.

The aircraft was flying level with the mountain tops and was at least a hundred kilometres off course.

All at once Kassner became aware of how very tiny he was, compared to the gigantic, stationary black mass of cloud; which did not look at all peaceful or stable perched up there; it looked alive and murderous, coiled ready to attack. Its edges were approaching the aircraft as if it had a hollowed-out centre into which the plane was flying, and its vastness, combined with the fact that everything seemed to be moving in slow motion, made the unfolding drama seem less like a prospective fight between two beasts than an inexorable, doom-laden process.

Yet the plane's wings tore into the storm-cloud at full tilt and, just like wave crests looming out of a low, sea-level fog, its frayed, smoky-yellow fringed tips merged into an endless, dark world of grey, a world without limits since it was completely cut off from the earth: the sombre, hemp-like cloud slipped past beneath them and spat them out into the open sky but that, too, was barricaded in by massive blocks of the same leaden bank of cloud. It suddenly occurred to Kassner that they had just escaped the pull of gravity, that he and the pilot were suspended in their cocoon of comradeship, out there among the galaxies, locked in a primitive combat with the monstrous hulk of cloud while, beneath them, earth and its dungeons travelled on, bound on a different course from theirs and their paths would never cross again. From the shadowy confines of the cabin and below, through the gaps in the engine's cowling, the vision of the tiny little aircraft, frenziedly dangling up there, buffeted by the angry clouds which had suddenly started fighting on their own terms, took on an unreal quality, overwhelmed as it was by the primeval howling of that powerful old enemy: the hurricane. Although the plane was pitching and abruptly dropping with every new squally gust as though it were plummeting to the ground, Kassner would only have concentrated on clinging to the machine that was blindly tugging them onwards, if the aircraft had not begun to sound as if it were frying: they were in the middle of a hailstorm.

"Czechoslovakia?" yelled Kassner.

Impossible to hear the reply. The drumming sound coming from the plane's fuselage was like a tambourine being banged, ringing out above the clattering of the hailstones against the cabin windows. They were beginning to come in through the slats in the engine's cowling, stabbing at both of their faces and making their eyes sting. In between spasmodically blinking his eyes, Kassner managed to make out the hailstones streaming down the windows, then bouncing off the steel grooves and disappearing into the raging shadows in a furious, whirling cloud. If one of the windows broke, it would be impossible to control the plane. But the pilot appeared oblivious to it all, he seemed to be steering blindly through the hailstorm, as if by pure instinct. Even so, Kassner leant against the window-frame as hard as he could, jamming it shut with his right hand. Now, though, creeping into the cabin, came all the prison-cell inscriptions, the screams, the sounds of knocking on walls and the desire for revenge, keeping them both company in their battle against the hurricane.

The plane was still supposed to be set on a course due South, but the compass's needle was now beginning to point to the East.

"Left!" yelled Kassner. No good. "Left!" He could hardly hear the sound of his own voice, he was being so buffeted, scratched and virtually engulfed by the whirling, clattering hailstones which drowned out his shouts as they lashed the plane like whips, rocking and tossing it about. With his free arm he signalled leftwards. He saw the pilot yank the joystick over as if to make a 90° turn. Immediately, he looked back at the compass: the plane was banking to the right. The controls were no longer responding properly.

Yet the plane still seemed to be plunging headlong into the squall as unerringly as a drilling-rod; but, in the midst of the raging fury all around them and despite its disabled controls, the persevering, steadfast engine vibrantly confirmed the compelling belief that man can still prevail over his circumstances. Then, suddenly, the plane began shuddering from one end to the other.

An abrupt jolt brought it up harshly short, making it seem to hang in the air — majestically motionless — poised there, engulfed by the raging hailstorm and the dense, dark fog which even now seemed to be reflecting his own black mood: and there in the midst of all this, it was the compass alone which was the only thing still connecting them to what had once been the earth. Slowly, it began to turn to the right, then a sudden, harsh gust sent it spinning round and round again until it had made a full circle. Twice. Three times. The plane was corkscrewing in flat spins and looping the loop bang in the centre of the cyclone. Yet the sensation of motionlessness persisted, the stubborn engine was fighting furiously to drag them out of the grips of the storm. It was the sight of the dial's spinning needle though, that made a far more intense impression upon him than any amount of physical discomfort: just like a paralysed person's flickering eyes convey the still living force within, so it showed that the aircraft was still full of life. Whirring around inaudibly, it was a visible manifestation of that fantastic, almighty mass of energy that was flinging them about: the same powerful living force that lashes trees and bends them double and, with infinite precision, the whole fury of the cosmos was being transmitted to them within the confines of its minute, sensitive dial. The plane carried on spinning. The pilot was hunched over the joystick, concentrating on it with all his might. His face no longer looked like a nervy sparrow's as it had done earlier however, it had become totally different: with smaller eyes and fuller lips, not deformed in any way though, it looked just as *natural* as the former one had; it was not a contorted mask at all — just a new, different kind of mask. Yet this came as no surprise to Kassner; as if the pilot's earlier expression had already given him a hint of the fact, he finally realised that this was the face of a child. It was not the first time (even if it was only at this moment the fact had struck him so clearly for the very first time) that, when he had witnessed someone calmly and resolutely facing danger, the man's face had been transformed and his expression had changed into a child-like mask. Suddenly, the pilot yanked back the joystick towards himself, the obstinate plane tilted its nose and began shooting upwards; then the compass's needle jammed against the glass face of the dial. They had been heaved upwards by a force from below, just like a sperm-whale being heaved belly-up by a tidal wave. The engine was still chugging on steadily but Kassner's stomach had sunk into his seat. Were they looping the loop or climbing vertically? He got his breath back between the next two bouts of lashings by the whipping hailstones. With a sense of shock he realised that he was shaking, it wasn't his hands (he was still holding the window-frame down) it was his left shoulder only that was trembling. He was just beginning to wonder if the plane was horizontal again when the pilot thrust the joystick forward and abruptly cut off the engine.

Kassner was familiar with this tactic: the trick was to drop down in free-fall, taking advantage of the increase in gravity caused by the plane's loss of altitude to break through the storm, then try to pull out and recover one's position nearer the ground. The altimeter was reading 1,850 metres but he knew one shouldn't rely too much on the accuracy of those gauges. Down to 1,600 already; the needle was jigging around like the compass's dial had been earlier on. If it was as foggy as this down at ground level, or if they were still flying over the mountains, they would crash. It occurred to Kassner that it was only when watching a man facing certain death one was allowed a glimpse of the child within, as he himself had been when looking at the pilot earlier, and that this man was even prepared to risk his life and die for him. At least they would die together. His shoulder had already stopped trembling now   the plane had ceased being a mere passive combatant in the struggle. Instead, he sensed that all his faculties had now become hyper-tuned, he felt acutely aroused in a distinctly sexual way: every one of his senses was tingling searingly, taking his breath away, piercing him through the blasts of wind like holes being torn in strips of canvas, amid the interminable fog in which the end of the world was being savagely played out in tune with the ear-splitting racket the hailstones were making.

1,000
950
920
900
870
850, his eyes felt as if they were starting out of his head, his eyes which were frantically and fearfully straining to catch sight of an approaching mountain — yet at the same time he felt utterly elated.

600
550
500

4... There it was... there was the plain — not horizontal and straight ahead like he had thought it would be, but far away in the distance and slanting at an angle! He was taken aback by the unreal sight of the horizon tilting at 45° (it was actually the plane that was dropping at an angle), but realising this he soon readjusted, while the pilot tried to level out from the dive and recover his line of flight. The earth was still far away, far beyond that vile ocean of malevolent clouds, seething with its maelstrom of dusty flakes and spiky horrors, which had already swallowed them up once more then parted again: and through its last remaining tattered wisps, a hundred metres below the plane, a lead-coloured landscape burst into view. Rocky, flinty-looking hills glinted darkly around a deathly pale lake which spread its sinuous tentacles out across the valley floor, and in which, with an eerie, geological calm, the lowering, lividly pale sky was serenely reflected.

"Czechoslovakia?" yelled Kassner once again.

"Don't know..."

Battered virtually to bits the plane trailed along beneath the storm, barely 50 metres above the peaks, then on above purple-tinged vineyards and on over the lake which was not nearly so calm as it had appeared at first sight. They could now see that the filmy, wide expanse of water was being whipped up into choppy little wavelets by a stiff surface-level wind. For the second time, Kassner felt that it was his wife who had been saved. The plane cleared the far side of the lake and fields, roads, factories and farms which, seen from that height, looked absolutely flat, with rivers snaking sinuously across the vast, scarred crust of the now recognisable plains, and everything, every single thing that was eternally symbolic of mankind's noble, defiant struggle against the earthly world rushed up towards Kassner. Every few seconds, as it all appeared then disappeared in a flash between the lowest clouds, he caught fleeting glimpses of the sum total of man's heroic existence, of his dogged battle for survival on that earth with its insatiable appetite for an endless diet of corpses. This world, growing darker by the minute, was laying bare its very soul to Kassner, pouring its heart out to him in as hollow, imperious tones as those of the cyclone now retreating behind them. All the indomitable will-power of his people who were fighting so desperately below somewhere beyond the Carpathians, struggling to overcome their fate and escape from bondage, welled up to meet the sky's last remaining rays of ruddy light, now harmonising with the divine tones of that vast luminous void — symbolising the very rhythm of life and death itself.

He let go of the window-frame, smiling as he caught sight of his palm with its line of life; it was long that one, and its line of fate which, ironically, he had etched himself with a razor-blade. His whole life and destiny had been carved out like those lines, not engraved with a razor like his line of fate had been, but shaped by his own tenacity and by the constantly patient efforts he had made; after all, what did man's freedom mean, if not his awareness of and the working-out of his own destiny? On that earth below, where more and more sparkling little lights were coming on, glowing as though they were literally rising up through the opaque mixture of autumnal mist and nightfall; on that earth full of dungeons and sacrifice, where acts of heroism had taken place, where selflessness and saintliness had existed, surely common decency and a moral conscience existed too, somewhere. The roads, rivers and canals which scarred the landscape were almost invisible now, becoming lost in the mist, the way the pattern of lines criss-crossing the palm of an enormous hand seem to have been gradually smoothed out. Kassner had heard that, when people die, the lines on the palms of their hands disappear and, immediately after his mother had died he had instantly examined one of her palms, as if to catch a final sign of life there before it finally vanished. Although she had been scarcely more than fifty years old and her face and even the backs of her hands had remained youthful-looking, her palm had already begun to look like an elderly woman's, with its fine, but deeply etched tracery of lines criss-crossing one another indiscriminately like the fateful paths of someone's destiny. It seemed to be merging now with the rest of those interlinking lines that covered the world below, becoming lost like them, in the mist and darkness and, like the others, those lines too had begun to look like the fateful paths of someone's destiny. The peacefulness of the ghostly-pale world below welled up towards the battered, worn-out plane which battled onwards through the rain that was still streaming down as though it were pursuing it like an echo of the hail and hurricane they had left behind. The world they were now rejoining seemed bathed in an atmosphere of infinite calm, with its fields and vineyards, its houses and its trees which were probably full of roosting, sleeping birds.

Kassner and the pilot exchanged glances. The latter gave an awkward, conspiratorial smile, like a schoolboy who has just avoided being punished for some misdemeanour; then he suddenly recognised one of the railway-tracks and began following it, buzzing up and down in the last shifting gusts of wind, just like an enormous bumble-bee.

The lights of Prague began to glimmer on the horizon.

CHAPTER VII

Oh, to be walking along that strangely unreal pavement just there, in this town where none of the roads lead to a German dungeon! As they drove past the dazzling array of shop windows his keyed-up senses played tricks on him, making them seem like the fantastic visions his imagination would conjure up when, as a child, he would come out of some children's show or other, his mind filled with fairytales: enormous streets, full of pineapples and pâtés and Chinese trinkets, where some evil spirit had conspired to line them with shops selling the entire range of Hell's tempting goodies... It was he himself, though, who had escaped from Hell and all this was simply everyday life carrying on as normal... He got out of the airport car.

The pilot had wanted to stay on at the airfield: he was leaving for Vienna the following day, with another comrade. Both he and Kassner were well acquainted with the deep bond that builds up between men who have shared traumatic experiences, and how profoundly affected they are by these feelings, so much so that when they are faced with everyday reality once more they are unable to express them, keeping them buried at the back of their minds. They had smiled resignedly at one another and just shaken hands.

Kassner returned to his life as a civilian as if he were going on a mind-numbingly long and deeply relaxing holiday; yet he was still unable to come to terms with either his own inner self or the real world he found himself in again. There was a woman doing her ironing behind some curtains, concentrating hard on doing it carefully; so shirts, household linen, and hot irons did exist in this strange place called earth... There were hands too (he was walking past the window of a glove shop), there were hands here that people used to do just about anything: there was nothing anywhere around him that hadn't been either made, touched or performed by them. This was a world peopled by hands, maybe they were even able to live and move by themselves, independent of their human owners. Everything was totally unrecognisable: he couldn't reconcile himself to all these ties, suitcases, sweets, the charcuteries' pork meats, these gloves, these chemists' shops and this furrier's shop window in which a little white dog was wandering about in the middle of the fur skins, sitting down then wandering off again: there, that was a living being, with its long fur and erratic movements, but it still wasn't a human. It was an animal. He'd forgotten all about animals. Yet here was the dog, calmly ambling around in the midst of death itself, in the very same way as all those passers-by, prison-fodder and cemetery-fodder the lot of them, were strolling towards the square. Here and there were gigantic music-hall posters with pictures of figures dressed in Prussian blue jigging about, and the passers-by walking beneath them seemed to be keeping in step with them. But underlying all this cheerfulness was another domain, an unseen world which stretched far and wide like a silent ocean, a world whose dying echoes still rumbled on in Kassner's mind: he was still punch-drunk from that experience of absolute nothingness, and having difficulty sobering up. Here were more grocers' shops full of provisions, clothes shops, now a greengrocer's. Oh, all these fruits, wonderfully redolent of the very breath of life itself! First though, he must find Anna again. All the same, he went into a tobacconist's, bought some cigarettes, lit one up immediately and once again drifted off into his fantasy world through the haze of smoke: here was a milliner's window, now a fancy leather-goods shop, a clock and watch-maker's (time too, was on sale, but these hours on display here were not dungeon-hours), a café now. People.

People still existed. People had carried on living while he'd descended into the pitch-dark realm of the blind. He watched them, with the same kind of emotional turmoil he'd felt when, during the war, he'd come across a window-display overflowing with trinkets, right at the end of a ruined alley-way full of blood-spattered rubble. Here, the working-class districts adjoined the poorest of the bourgeois neighbourhoods... Were these some of his own people here, or enemies, or other people who had nothing to do with him and couldn't care less about him? Some of them seemed happy to be together in the quite friendly, warmish atmosphere, others, either patiently or vehemently, were trying to extract a bit more attention out of the person they were talking to; and there were all those worn-out feet littering the ground, and quite a bit of hand-holding and finger-intertwining going on underneath the table-tops. This was life.

This was people's everyday life in its tiniest humdrum detail; and, hey, there were three women standing over there by the door; one of them was really beautiful: something in her expression looked just like Anna's. So women existed too, here on earth; but his weakened state had left him chaste, rather than sexually obsessed. All the same, he yearned to touch them, like he'd wanted to stroke the dog: but within the last nine days his hands had become almost lifeless. Behind him, though, men were still screaming out loud in cells somewhere and a man had sacrificed himself for him. Oh, how absurd it was to call only those people who have blood-ties, "brothers". He immersed himself in the lukewarm flood of the potty, idiotic phrases and exclamations going on around him, in the talkers' very breathing even, as if basking in the crazy marvellous warmth of life itself; he felt intoxicated by fellow-feeling for mankind. Had he been killed this morning, perhaps this would have been the everlasting vision he would have carried with him into the hereafter: this humid period of an autumn day from which the bustle of people's daily life seemed to drift slowly up into the air, like mist condensing in tiny droplets upon ice-cold glasses. The world's comedy of everyday life and manners was ushering in the intense peacefulness of dusky twilight; women, fragrant with their special perfumes for evening strolls, were grouped around shop windows... Oh, blessed peace of evenings devoid of prison-dungeons, of evenings when there was nobody dying nearby! Maybe he'd come back here on an evening such as this after he really had been killed?

Out there in the darkness the whole countryside was at rest, with its tall apple-trees standing erect, surrounded by their rings of dead apples; with its mountains and forests, and half the entire world full of animals deep in their interminable slumbering. And here were these crowds of people surging around, zestfully living life to the full, sporting their smiling, night-time expressions or collapsing and dying elsewhere, meeting death with its wreaths and coffins. This crazy, carefree throng was rushing around, totally unaware of what inner potential each one of them possessed, of what resources they could draw upon when confronted by death, which lay in wait for them, hiding up there in the star-studded steppes of the heavens. The teeming crowd carried on headlong: deaf to its own inner voice, unaware even of its passionate soul, which did in fact exist despite being left unheeded thanks to the careless, incessant bustle that Kassner was rediscovering, just as he was going to be reunited with his wife and child once more.

He reached his house. Went up the stairs. Was he going to find himself back in his dungeon? He knocked on his door. No reply. He knocked again, louder, then saw a card stuck in the bottom corner of the door: "I'm at Lucerna". Anna was an activist who campaigned among the German exiles' circles and Lucerna was one of the largest assembly-halls in Prague. He'd have to buy the Party's newspaper. He looked at the door, stunned and utterly desolate, yet at the same time feeling a sense of overwhelming relief: she'd obviously been aware of his arrest, and he had never been able to think about their eventual reunion without dreading it. Wasn't his child asleep on the other side of that stupid door? No, obviously not, otherwise he'd have been woken by the knocking. Besides, she wouldn't have left him all by himself.

When he'd been set free, and again when the plane had escaped from the storm, he'd felt that it was she, and not he, who'd been saved; now, he felt cheated by her absence. He went back downstairs and bought the paper: Theatres... Cinemas... Lucerna: *Rally for the imprisoned anti-Fascists*. There was a rally every week. By going to that at least she was with him in spirit.

There were between fifteen and twenty thousand men assembled there and although the atmosphere was reminiscent of a world championship or a fair, it was also heavy with imminent danger: they were surrounded by police standing on street corners, lights glinting off their guns. Because the main hall was too small to hold so many people, loud-speakers had been installed all around the building. After having some trouble getting inside, Kassner found that everyone near him had their heads tilted backwards, noses in the air, listening to the harsh, rasping sounds coming from the megaphones.

"... My son was a worker. He wasn't even a Socialist. They sent him to the Oranienburg prison-camp[27] and he died there."

It was a woman's voice speaking. Once Kassner had finally managed to get through to the main hall, he was able to make out the shape of an elderly woman standing at the very centre of the converging banks of scarlet, slogan-covered banners and leaning awkwardly over the microphone: she was wearing an unremarkable mass-produced type of hat and a black coat — obviously dressed in her Sunday best. Below her he could only see the backs of people's necks, which all looked identical: he'd never be able to find Anna among such an enormous crowd of people.

"... Because he went to an anti-Fascist demonstration, just before the others seized power...

"I'd never bothered with politics before that. People say that politics is none of women's business. Dead children, that's their business...

"I'm... I'm not... going to make a speech..."

Kassner was familiar with the agonies suffered by someone who was unused to addressing a large audience, who freezes when their first rush of emotion runs out, then dries up completely as they are overcome by the expectant audience's own excitement (besides, many of those who were listening to her did not understand German) almost as if the speaker were staggering beneath the onslaught of a massive, but voiceless response. Nevertheless, this interruption had the same kind of powerful effect upon the listeners as when the howls of animals being slaughtered break off abruptly the moment their throats are slit: determined not to let matters rest there, the crowd was now craning their necks forward and panting even harder than the old woman was. One would have thought it was their very own consciences that were being called into question. Kassner began to wonder how all this was going down outside in the street where only the panting sound was being transmitted over the loudspeakers — and where Anna, perhaps, was listening to it as well. By now he had got to within three metres of the rear of the platform and was straining hard to catch sight of her among the thousands of other faces in front of him. He felt giddy.

"Say we won't stand for it," said another woman under her breath.

She was whispering, just like one does at school. Along with the rest of the crowd she was waiting, chin jutted forward, for the words that were sticking in their throats to be finally uttered out loud. The other woman did not move and Kassner watched the speechless old "Mother Fury's" motionless back while the crowd muttered, softly prompting her to call for revenge. Seeing the anguished faces of the audience in front of her he guessed that she was at a loss for words. She was gradually stooping lower and lower, as if she needed to pluck the phrases she was searching for off the floor.

"They killed him... that's all I have to say to people... Anything else... Well, the delegates and cleverer people than me, people who know all about these things are going to speak in a minute... they'll explain it all to you..."

She raised her fist in the air, was probably going to shout "Red Front" as if she were used to seeing people doing that, but because her self-assurance had deserted her to the point where she was almost choking with the effort, she only managed to raise her arm slightly and pronounced the two words in an undertone, her voice tailing away as though she were signing off at the end of a letter. Everyone there was on her side, at one with her in her discomfiture, seeing their own awkwardness mirrored in hers and, as she shrank back and retreated towards the rear of the platform, waves of encouraging applause rose towards her in the same way her suffering had reached out and touched them when she had been voicing her own grief. Then, as emotion gave way to sounds of coughing and nose-blowing and while the Chairman was translating into Czech — reaction, then relief, set in and people started looking around anxiously for something more cheerful to think about. Did this general restlessness mean that Kassner would finally be able to catch sight of Anna, with those eyes of hers that had always reminded him of Siamese cats?

Suddenly, only twenty metres away from where he was standing, he glimpsed her vaguely mulatto-like face and, framed by their long black eyelashes, those eyes, filled with their enormous limpid pupils. He elbowed his way frantically past masses of backs and chests towards her: it was a stranger, some young woman he did not know, who was saying "... forbidden to play war-games and the last time he came home with a black eye he explained: 'we're more civilised now, you see, we're playing at revolutions'..." He inched his way forward, painfully scared of imagining that anyone who remotely resembled Anna from a distance was in fact her: "We're bound to be able to raise some money if they put blokes from the building trade in the delegation — Why don't we?" It was very hot in there. He'd scrutinised so many faces by now, had soaked in so many details, he began to wonder if he'd ever be able to recognise his wife again. He went back nearer the platform. A secretary was dictating instructions for the campaign to one of the comrades:

"Ambassadors and consuls must be constantly telephoned by people demanding the prisoners' release. — You must set up permanently manned committee-rooms. — You must establish Commissions of Inquiry in Germany. — Postmen, you're to stick the Thälmann stamp[28] onto anything that's posted to Germany. — Sailors and dockers, carry on banning the Hitlerite flag from being flown in any port, get into conversation with German sailors. — Railwaymen, you're to paint our slogan on the wagons bound for Germany..."

Eventually, the Chairman's voice could be heard, speaking in a conversational tone:

"Little Wilhelm Schradek, who is seven years old, has lost his father who can collect him from the office," then, slightly louder: "I'll hand you over now to Comrade..."

A name was given followed by a sentence Kassner did not understand. However, all the chatting had abruptly died down and waves of silence spread outwards in ever-increasing circles from around the odd pockets of noise, gradually muffling the occasional ripple of applause.

"Comrades, listen to all the cheering and clapping going on out there in the dark...
"Can you hear how much there is and how it's coming from so far away..."
"How many of us are there, standing here packed into these assembly-rooms, like sardines? Twenty thousand. Comrades, there are more than one hundred thousand men shut away in prisons and concentration camps over there in Germany..."

Obviously Kassner was not going to be able to find Anna, even if he felt close to her, in among that crowd. The bald little man who was now speaking and who must have been an intellectual, judging by the kind of language he was using, was holding forth without gesticulating, his only movement being to tug occasionally at his droopy moustache. The political delegates were evidently going to speak last.

"Our enemies spend millions on propaganda: we would not be doing our cause any harm if we expended the same amount of our own will-power on our efforts as they do with their money."

"We have managed to get Dimitrov[29] released. We'll continue pressing for the release of our other comrades who are in prison. People rarely kill for sheer pleasure alone, so they have been imprisoned for a reason. This is a method of discouraging opposition to the Nazi government, by intimidating protesters and suppressing any such opposition; but it so happens that the government has to reckon with foreign public opinion. If it becomes too unpopular it will cost it dear: this will prejudice its supply of arms and will damage its chances of obtaining any loans. We must not let up in our constant efforts to make the public aware of the truth. We must keep at it stubbornly and remorselessly, because we have to ensure that Hitler loses more than he gains by carrying on with what he calls repression."

Kassner's mind went back to the speech he had delivered into the shadows of his cell.

"Putting Dimitrov publicly on trial was unwise, because then they had to let him be seen in public. Then acquitted. The Cologne prosecutor is wrong when he triumphantly crows: 'Once again justice has taken up its sword and the executioner has picked up his axe, just as it used to be', but the axe which mirrors the unknown militants' faces is also making those very faces known to the public. What is more, whether it is Thälmann or Torgler, Ludwig Renn or Ossietzky,[30] day by day all these men and others are slowly approaching the moment when they will go through what has always been man's ultimate, noblest experience, as surely as all life journeys inexorably towards certain death..."

For Kassner, the faces of those just mentioned began to mingle with those of all the men locked up in prison-cells, merging together in a world far removed from the one where this speech was being heard. Now, as he watched, in the very same way as when he had seen the pilot's expression change into the typical child-like mask of a man gripped in the jaws of Death, so he saw the crowd's faces transformed before his very eyes: momentarily distracted from their common cause, the will to action, their faces were becoming suffused with the passionate sincerity and deep emotions one can only witness among similar large gatherings of men. This was exactly the same kind of exhilaration someone feels in wartime when the fighter squadrons take off and one's plane is tearing down the runway between two others towards lift-off, with pilots and lookouts alike focusing their whole attention upon the battle ahead. Yet, at the very moment he was rediscovering this numbingly solemn, but fierce feeling of affinity with his fellow-men, thoughts of his invisible wife, too, came into his mind.

"German comrades, you who have sons or brothers locked up in concentration camps, this very night, at this very minute, there are masses of people similar to ourselves, gathered together at meetings like ours, from here to Spain and even as far away as the Pacific, maintaining their vigil across the entire world, keeping faith with those lone men in their solitude..."

It was because they too were keeping faith with their own people walled up in German prisons that this enormous crowd had chosen to be here. It was not for amusement, nor because they had nothing else to do and were bored; they were here because of what they already knew and what they still did not know about and wanted to know. And it was their passionately resolute response, including the unseen Anna's too no doubt, that underscored this rousing speech which resonated with hollow echoes of man's infinite suffering and provided an answering blow on behalf of the prisoner who had been battered senseless against the wall. Everyone was waiting for their cue. Kassner had often wondered whether it was any use having the capacity for thought and feelings since having been faced with those two Siberian corpses, with their crushed genitalia, lying there with butterflies flitting around their faces. Cruelty was the lowest, most extreme form of human expression, unlike any other; but virile fraternity and solidarity in the face of evil existed too, faced up to it on equal terms, at the very core of man's being, and confronted it in the inner sanctum of men's souls, even when those very souls conceal the lurking threat of torture and death...

CHAPTER VIII

He lit a cigarette, the twelfth since the aerodrome, as if to light up the stairway, which was now in darkness. The door of his apartment was ajar. He pushed it open and went inside. There was nobody in the study but he could hear the sound of voices coming from the second room, although there was no strip of light showing beneath the door. The shutters had not been opened. Keeping his finger on the light-switch, he listened to the voice, which seemed muffled by the faint haze in the room and at the same time clarified by the reflections of the street-lights filtering into the gloom of the study where the large, pale shape of a tapestry hanging on a wall loomed out of the shadows:

"My little one, my little bundle of joy, my little spring chicken! Chicken? I gave you such a gorgeous pair of eyes, as blue as blue, and if they're not enough for you, I'll give you some Sunday-worshipper's eyes.[31] If I give you those kind of eyes we'll go and see the land of the baby animals. That's where there are lots of dogs and birds, and they're all fluffy and furry, because they're very young and tiny; and there are fishes and ladyfishes there too, with mouths like dandelion clocks. But they're oh, so blue! And we'll see tiny little kittens and bear-cubs there too. And we'll tiptoe everywhere, the two of us."

Then suddenly, as though she had been struck by something, her voice changed and she repeated, sadly:

"Just the two of us, only the two..."

The child was chirping and cooing in reply. Anna was there, on the other side of the room, in the dark too, and Kassner's heart gradually swelled and feasted on this invisible manifestation of motherliness.

"You'll see the sad little fishes who live far away in the deep sea. They have little lanterns so they can find their way around. And when they feel too cold..."

She tried to think of something.

"They go off and hide in the land of furry fishes," said Kassner softly as he pushed open the door.

She had clutched the back of her chair and was nervously shaking her head from side to side as if denying both the fact that Kassner had come in and that furry fish really existed. He smiled, a kind of frozen smile which he could feel stretching across his face like a wound tightening the skin as it heals over. The light coming through the window was casting the shadow of a large, black cross onto the base of Anna's neck where it trembled on her quivering skin; Kassner realised that her knees too were knocking, rather like shuddering shoulders, beneath her skirt. She got up, still unable to stop clinging to the back of her chair as if she had become attached to it. She finally let go and stretched her hand towards the light-switch but could not bring herself to touch it; he sensed that she was frightened of seeing his face in the light.

Making any gestures or saying anything would be inadequate and would not ring true, would be pathetically absurd above all — too brusque and meaninglessly shallow — a virtual parody of their true, deeper feelings. It would be better to remain silent and keep absolutely still and for neither of them to touch the other one at all, which was always more meaningful than an embrace; but neither of them could and they kissed each other.

"What... what was it like?" she asked as she drew away from his embrace.

"Dreadful," he said, simply.

He stroked the child's head and felt its cheek seeking his hand. He hardly knew the little features at all: he could only clearly remember its expressions and, in his eyes, the tiny child had not existed for him as a real human being until it had smiled for the first time two days before he had left. He relished the hopes he had for this little life, but above all he relished the animal-like, complete and utter confidence the child had in him: one day when he had rapped his knuckles because he had been tugging the dog's hairs, the little one had still thrown himself into his arms. The child was a bundle of trust, from his sleepy cheek nestling in his father's hand to his untroubled dreams, and for him alone, he, Kassner, meant only a world of happiness. "This time yesterday..." Kassner gently withdrew his hand, held it in front of his eyes and looked at his five fingers in the gloomy half-light. His nail had probably barely grown at all yet. They went into the study. She turned round:

"Did they fall for the fake identity, in the..."

He had just switched on the light. She had instinctively recoiled, throwing back her shoulders; ...surely not:

"I was so afraid that..." she said.

His face had seemed worn and ravaged in the glow of the cigarette alone. Now, in the light she could see that, although he had lost weight, his naturally bony face had actually changed very little. She knew enough from the letters she had seen from other prisoners' wives who had not recognised their husbands, particularly from those who had been told to "Bring some clean laundry", because their old shirt was soaked through with blood and ruined — to "have been very afraid".

"Did they fall for your fake identity?" she asked for the second time.

He sensed that face to face with him now, Anna was asking him those very same questions she had been asking herself again and again, for days on end, while she had been all alone.

"No. Well, not at first. Then somebody confessed, claiming he was Kassner."

She raised her eyes to his and the pointed silence that ensued was so acute all he could say was:

"No, I don't know who it was..."

She sat down on the divan by the window. She did not speak for a while but sat contemplating him in such a manner it seemed almost as though she felt a part of him had stayed and died with the man who had given himself up back there.

"Killed?"

"I don't know..."

"I've got so much to tell you," she said; "but at the moment I still can't seem to be able to speak properly. We ought to just talk about any old thing, something superficial for the time being... until I've got used to having you actually here with me..."

He knew that he really ought to take her quietly in his arms, and making a silent gesture like that would be the only way he could show her what a deep bond linked them both with their dead comrade, but he had never been one for traditional demonstrations of tenderness even if there are no other appropriate kinds of gesture to make in such circumstances.

"How is he?" asked Kassner, nodding towards the room where the child was now asleep.

She inclined her head in turn, in a sad yet bemused manner, as if she were marvelling at the fact that, however much she tried to appear radiant and full of happiness, however much she tried to speak normally, her tone of voice would belie her true feelings and she would not be able to express how much love she felt for her child without betraying just how much grief her other love caused her.

It was the first time in the five years they had been living together that Kassner had returned home from so far away; but he had heard all about the kinds of homecoming which were marred by the prospect of yet another parting. Even though she was trying so hard, if in vain, to hide how sad she really felt and to put on a happy face and pretend to accept her lot, and despite the sorrow which made her press herself so closely against him, the knowledge that he was the cause of so much pain somehow made him feel dreadfully remote from her. Even though she might accept his going away and rationally and wholeheartedly endorse what he was doing, even though she campaigned actively for the cause as and when possible, none of all this made the slightest difference. He sometimes wondered if, in her heart of hearts, she might not reproach him for having a life in which anything that happened took place in a world far removed from that of her own private grief — a grief she never openly acknowledged but quietly endured with humble desperation. He was not unaware of how much he sometimes resented her for the fact that he loved her so very much.

"When the plane was taking off, there were dozens of leaves swirling around like whirlwinds underneath us. Joy is a bit like that, like flurries of featherweight leaves... skipping along, on the surface..."

There was something rather cruel in being dismissive about joy at the very moment she was clearly wanting to be the very embodiment of joyfulness for him; but she had guessed by what he had just said that he did feel for her and identified with her suffering and, in her mind, anything they felt in common and which brought them closer to one another could never hurt her:

"If only I could give you some joy..." she said.

She sensed that he felt ill at ease and gave a gentle shake of her head as if to say "no", but with such sadness still and being so delicately tactful in her very gaucheness, it made him realise yet again how crude and coarse men always are when faced with genuine tenderness.

"My life is what it is. I've accepted it, I even... chose it... I just want you to keep a little place in your life for me: but something occurred to me and I wanted to say that I would like to make you feel much more joyful..."

The husband of one of her friends, who had come back home after being in a concentration camp, used to wake up nearly every night screaming "Don't hit me!" Kassner had closed his eyes, making Anna remember how nowadays she was afraid of going to sleep.

"There are times," she said, "when I feel that it's not so much the nature of suffering that changes, it's the nature of hope..."

She raised her limpid eyes, looking up through her long black eyelashes, to meet his. Her brow furrowed as she slowly looked him up and down. Feeling like someone coming round from a faint and slowly regaining consciousness, Kassner saw her intelligent-looking face with its changing expressions loom before him and come into focus. How well he knew her variety of expressions, how every change of mood, however secret it was, flitted across her face, the way everyone's face reflects their hidden thoughts; he'd so often witnessed her tears, her love and her sensuality reflected on her face, and these characteristic expressions of hers at times could even become the very picture of joy itself for him. Whatever humiliation he might have suffered in his prison-dungeon, if these eyes had been able to witness it they would only have done so in order to share it with him. While she was speaking, he saw the pain and the lines gradually disappear from her face:

"I've made up so many imaginary conversations with you that I've always been afraid of the moment I'd wake up. But I promised myself though, that when the day came I would not say anything that seemed the tiniest bit sad to you. I'm more joyful inside than..."

She could not find the words to go on and smiled, making a slight gesture with her hand, her old smile coming back again at last, while her wonderful teeth flashed, lighting up her face. Finally, with a hint of bitterness, she said:

"but I don't dare show it...", as if she were still afraid.

She had not dared to say anything like that until now; was it still too soon for them to be contemplating the very idea of happiness? Life was slowly drawing him back into its embrace, just as his arm was encircling her body, slowly taking hold of him once more.

"Maybe," she said, "I'm thinking carefully about every word I'm going to say today before saying it, because I can't think any other way at the moment, but that doesn't mean to say I'm wrong to do that. I'm not always a very happy person anyway: I don't have a very easy life, in fact it's very difficult... But the most important thing that keeps me going in life is knowing that child is there. That he's mine. There must be at least five thousand, I don't know, maybe even ten thousand children in this town. And thousands of women who are going to start going into labour in a few minutes' time (the pains usually start coming at about one or two in the morning) and who are waiting... expectantly. They may be full of fear; but they feel something else as well. The word joy is meaningless compared with that kind of feeling. So is any other word. It's always been like that, ever since the beginning of the world and of time, it's been like that every night."

He could tell by her words that her innate delicacy and perhaps some vague superstitious fear were prompting her to use the only images she had managed to cling on to after so many anxiety-ridden months, to express her feelings of joy. The child's voice broke into their thoughts: he wasn't crying, only talking to himself.

"You were in Germany when he was born. I woke up and saw him lying there, looking so puny and defenceless in his cradle, then I thought that life would turn out for him the way life always turns out for everyone and I burst into tears, blubbering for him and his life and for myself and my life... I was so weak the tears wouldn't stop streaming down my face but from that very moment on I knew that I had something apart from pain and sorrow in my life..."

"Men don't give birth."

He could not tear his eyes away from this face he had believed was dead.

"Still, when they're shut away in dungeons, you see, they have this incredible need for something to be there, something meaningful which will help them hold out against their awful suffering... Joy can't be put into words."

"At least music gave me some joy."

"I can't stand music now."

She was just going to ask why but, instinctively, thought the better of it. He sensed that she was listening to him with her body as much as with her mind, listening to him like a mother listens, understanding what he was really meaning to say before hearing the words he was using to try and explain his feelings. It occurred to him, in a confused way, that in spite of the prison-cells and all the cruelty which existed in the world, in spite of all that, man had succeeded in preserving his sense of self and that maintaining one's dignity in the face of extreme pain was almost certainly the only solution... But he didn't want to think any more, he just wanted to go on looking at Anna.

There was a sudden sound of knocking on a neighbouring door. Kassner immediately began hearing the knocking that had gone on in the prison again: but it had made her jump even more than him:

"I thought that was you coming home!"

They heard a door open and the sound of people warmly greeting each other. That was a real door, opening in the real world, and those were real human voices...

"I'd like to start writing again," he said. "When I was locked up alone in my cell, I tried thinking of music... and using it as a kind of self-defence — for hours on end. Naturally, it set off a load of memories and flashbacks — and, strangely, one of the lines from the caravan-drivers' invocations stuck in my mind: "If this should be a night of destiny...""

She took hold of his hand and pressed the back of it to her temple; then she took his face and, holding it against her, began caressing it:

"... Blessed be this night until the coming of the dawn...," she murmured.

She had averted her gaze and was looking out into the darkness; he could barely see her profile through the hand she was still holding in hers. It had been raining and a car was passing by on the road outside, making a noise like leaves rustling in the wind as it drove along the wet surface of the road. He could see Anna's eye, still half-obscured by his hand but now framed by the window, looking over to the corner between two deserted streets. Kassner instantly knew that the image of that house on the corner would stay in his mind for ever.

In a low voice, Anna said:

"All the same, the next time you go off I want... less hard than you might think..."

She had wanted to say: to accept it. The house had six windows, three on each side — and two skylights; they were all in darkness, but were still paler than the sky because of some reflection coming off the glass which was still glistening from the rain, and night was gently exuding its soothing, all-enveloping calm just as Anna's arms had enfolded him so soothingly earlier.

The house seemed held in the thrall of one of those mystical moments which make mankind believe that a god has just been born. A child ran out and disappeared into the darkness. Kassner felt that, even if his mind was still stuck in a blood-stained time-warp because of all the trauma he'd been through, this was a new dawn: the true meaning of life was being created there and then and the most secret purpose of every material object's existence was about to be unveiled and thus fulfilled. He shut his eyes: the sense of touch was far more penetratingly effective than any other of the senses, even more incisive than the power of thought itself, and the feeling of Anna's temple against his fingers felt singularly in harmony with the hushed peacefulness that had descended upon the world. He could see himself again, back there in his dungeon, running around — counting: one, two, three, four... — trying to reassure himself that she was alive.

He reopened his eyes straightaway and it dawned upon him that he could be holding their entire future within his grasp, a future that would be created and forever transformed by what had happened in the past, with yesterday's prisoners, with the infant's trusting cheek, with the crowds keeping faith with their tortured comrades, with the pilot's face in the hurricane, with the prisoner who had sacrificed himself for him, Kassner; it would even be influenced by his next sortie into Germany. It would be a future forever filled with life and living people, not the eternity that awaited the dead. This vision of the future embraced all this and swept everything before it, throbbing through his veins to fuse with man's unique inmost potential, which enables him to transcend his humanity: his innate gift of virile courage. It rained down, pounding the newly deserted street outside where the wind was beginning to get up again. Every future act he, Kassner, would carry out would be motivated by whatever was left of his blood-ties with those he loved, and this precious moment he was living right now would remain with him until the day it was snuffed out when he would meet his death in Germany. He suddenly felt that he couldn't bear to remain still any longer:

"I feel like going for a walk, going out with you somewhere, anywhere."

"I'll have to go and find someone to look after the little one."

She went out. He switched off the light, letting the earth's peaceful darkness flood into the room, looked out again at the two still empty streets a cat was bounding across, not prancing playfully, but streaking along, its paws scissoring mechanically, like a scampering mouse.

They would be able to talk properly to each other now, to swap memories and talk about things that had happened... Everything would return to normal and they could go back to their everyday life again. Together once more, they would walk downstairs side by side, go out and walk along streets, together, beneath the unchanging sky that had forever looked as it did at this moment, ever since mankind's spirit and will had either been extinguished or, against all odds, had emerged triumphant.

NOTES TO THE TEXT

[The notes refer to our translation. Where relevant, the corresponding words/phrases from the original French text are shown in bracketed italics after the English version.]

Author's Preface

1. **A devotee of Alexandrines,** *(Alexandrin)*: a writer of alexandrines, the twelve-syllable lines of verse which became the most common metre in French versification from the 16th century onwards, particularly favoured by the 17th century 'Classical' writers of poetry and drama; the 'Romantics' and 'Symbolists' of the 19th century used a looser form of alexandrine.

Chapter I

2. **The Electrozavod:** the main 'Electrical Factory' or 'Electricity Generating Board'. As Russia emerged from the aftermath of the devastating 1917 Revolution, she embarked upon a long-term planned economy, which included significant industrial development and a ten-year plan for the electrification of the whole country under the GOELRO State Commission, (measures which were strongly supported by Lenin and the Left).

3. **The German Volga Republic** *(la république allemande de la Volga)*: a region in S.E. Russia (the Ukraine) with a significant population of Germans who settled there as farmers (later prospering and becoming politicised), during the wide-scale multi-ethnic migrations which took place in Northern Europe (and what later became the U.S.S.R.) in the nineteenth century.

4. **Cell** *(cellule)*: a unit-group of workers, dissidents, etc; within a larger organisation.

5. **Moabit:** a district lying between Wedding and Tiergarten in North West Berlin. Originally donated to expatriate French Huguenots who fled France during the 17th century, the desolate barren land, now part of Greater Berlin, was christened 'Terre Maudite' (later Germanicised to 'Moabit') by the French immigrants. Once settled, the Huguenots' renowned manufacturing skills and trading expertise helped transform the area which became the birthplace of Berlin's industrial revolution. The heavily industrialised district was obviously a convenient location for dissident political activity in the early part of the 20th century; in fact the Communist Party set up their headquarters in Berlin.

6. **The SA:** the *Sturmabteilung:* storm-troopers, also known as "Brownshirts". These were members of the para-military wing (as opposed to the exclusively security and policing wing — the SS) of Hitler's own Nazi army, formed in the 1920s as his National Socialist movement stepped up its activities during his political campaign. Both the SA and the SS were banned in April 1932 by Brüning's government, but the ban was lifted later that year.

7. **Papen's decree** *(le décret Papen)*: Kassner is most probably alluding here to the emergency decree issued by Franz von Papen's government in September, 1932. It was designed to radically reorganise the German economy, nationalising coal and steel in the process, thereby alleviating the worst of the country's social and economic problems, which had become aggravated during the long period of political and social unrest that had plagued Germany since the late 1920s. The decree proved extremely unpopular, provoking widespread unrest in the industrial regions, including the Rühr (scene of a major revolt in 1920) with its mines, coal and steel industries.

8. **The "Red Relief"** *(Le Secours Rouge)*: almost certainly a reference to the All-Russia Famine Relief Committee formed in July 1921 to provide aid and welfare to victims of the famine which had affected 20% of the population, victims of the many years of peasant wars in addition to those of the main 1917 Revolution.

9. **The Siberian Civil War** *(la guerre civile sibérienne)*: Siberia and other regions were the scenes of wide-scale bitter and bloody conflicts when civil war broke out in Russia in April 1918 between the "Reds", (Trotsky's Workers' and Peasants' Red Army, comprising many former Imperial Army Officers among other recruits) the army of the Communist Bolshevik Party, and the "Whites", the counter-revolutionary forces. The White army included many ex-tsarist officers and had its main bases in Siberia and the south of the country; it was better equipped than the Red Army but eventually lost the war, which ended in 1921.

10. **Hagen:** a town lying to the S. East of Essen in the Northern Rhine / Westphalia region of Germany.

Chapter II

11. **The Whites** *(les Blancs)*: see note 9 above.

12. *Isba*: the type of country or peasant's cottage later favoured as a second home or country retreat by wealthier members of the Russian population and now more commonly known as a "Dacha".

13. **Gelsenkirchen:** a large town lying to the north of Essen (see above) in the heavily industrialised and mining Rühr district.

14. **The Red Lancers** *(les Lances Rouges)*: the artillery regiments of the Red Army (see note 9 above).

15. **Tartar camel-train drivers sprawling prostrate out in the dusty Gobi desert** *(chameliers tartares prosternés... du Gobi)*: the former Russian Empire embraced many now independent nation-states e.g. Armenia. It is interesting to note that in Central Asia, before the 1917 Revolution, particularly in the Tartar regions, apart from political unrest and repression there was also considerable religious activity. The Russian Orthodox Church embarked upon a widespread campaign to convert the Tartars, also many Mongols and Moslems, to Christianity, more often than not by the use of force. The Russian Empire began to disintegrate, with uprisings in Central Russia, during the autumn of 1917.

16. **Bakunin** *(Bakounine)*: Mikhail Bakunin (1814-76), one of the early Russian revolutionaries who co-founded the Russian Populist Movement. He was exiled to and imprisoned in Siberia after taking part in the revolutionary struggles of 1848; later he escaped and fled to London to join other Communist exiles. He became a member of the First International association which aimed to unite globally all Socialist and Communist organisations. He later disagreed with Karl Marx, who was convinced that the existing political and social capitalist-orientated system would gradually become unviable, whereas Bakunin believed that matters could only deteriorate further under the Tsarist regime, and only revolution and violence would put an end to the social and political oppression of the workers and peasants.

Chapter III

17. **His wife's in Prague**: a second, but now semi-delirious allusion to Kassner's wife who has stayed with their child in Prague and is also a Communist militant. The ancient city of Prague in N.W. Czechoslovakia is in the region formerly known as the Sudetenland, which had been settled by German immigrants over several centuries and by the turn of the 19th/20th century contained a substantial population of the settlers' descendants and other German nationals. Hence, no doubt, Kassner and his family's presence there, although he himself is from Munich; not to mention the convenient distance from major German cities of Prague, from where he could make his sorties as an undercover agent. (After the First World War Sudetenland had been declared part of Czechoslovakia but was occupied by Hitler's Third Reich in 1938).

18. **The priests... this marching treasure trove...**, *(les popes... ce Trésor en marche)*: see notes 9 and 15. As Kassner sinks deeper into a state of semi-delirium punctuated by a series of flashbacks evoked by the melodies, he becomes obsessed by a vision of a procession of Russian Orthodox priests and ecclesiastical paraphernalia. This vision has in turn been conjured up by an association of images tied in with the antique collector's shop with its religious bric-à-brac, where he and his fellow Communist militants used to meet, and where the incident leading to his arrest took place.

19. **The Altai** *(L'Altaï)*: a mountainous area in central Asia, extending into Soviet Siberia and Mongolia.

20. *"Escargot"*: (literally "snail" in English). This "term" has not been translated since it is certainly a visual pun intended by Malraux to illustrate the partisan-sympathiser Kassner's dislike of affluent Russian society's penchant for over-ornate furniture and design. The image of the snail's spiral carapace epitomises the frequently elaborate, bulbous or scroll-like fantastic forms (sometimes perceived as grotesque), which are characteristic of Baroque furniture and architecture.

21. **Garments... costumes out of the Tales of Hoffmann**, *(Des frusques de Contes d'Hoffmann)*: the allusion to Offenbach's phantasmagorical operetta in which the eponymous hero "lives out" a dream love-affair in a fantasy world is well in keeping with the fantastic chaos described here as the partisans deck themselves out in the remnants of the ornate brocade garments.

22. **The Cossacks:** of South Russian origin and renowned for their horsemanship over the centuries, mostly sided with the Tsarists against the Bolsheviks during the 1917 Revolution.

Chapter V

23. **The old "Hall of Nobility"** *(la Salle de la Noblesse)*: the mausoleum in Moscow's Red Square, in which Lenin's body lay in state after his death in 1924.

24. **My companions... in China** *(mes compagnons de Chine)*: either an allusion to the war between Russia and China in Manchuria which ended in 1903, or, more possibly, to the massacre of Communist revolutionaries in Shanghai in 1927.

25. **Five million people still voted "no" during the plebiscite** *(il y a eu cinq millions de non au plébiscite)*: an allusion to the sham elections to the Reichstag in November 1933.

Chapter VI

26. **Transmitter** *(T.S.F.)*: The French term being an abbreviation of "Télégraphie sans Fil", i.e. wireless/radio set.

Chapter VII

27. **The Oranienburg prison-camp** *(le camp d'Oranienburg)*: site of the notorious concentration camp. Following the Reichstag fire in February 1933 Hitler, by then Chancellor since January, intensified his efforts at creating a country-wide Nazi (National Socialist) state and at repressing any opposition. The Social Democrat and Communist parties, the main political opposition, were declared illegal and two new concentration camps as opposed to mere slave-labour camps were built, at Dachau and Oranienburg, to house those who opposed the regime and other "undesirables". The infamous Sachsenhausen concentration camp, then "officially" a labour camp and larger than the preceding camp, was built at Oranienburg in 1937.

28. **The Thälmann stamp** *(le timbre Thaelmann)*: an "unofficial" stamp issued to commemorate Ernst Thälmann, the chairman of the German Communist Party, the K.P.D. *(Kommunistische Partei Deutschlands)* who, among other K.P.D. deputies, was arrested immediately after the Reichstag fire.

29. **Dimitrov** *(Dimitroff)*: Georgi Dimitrov (1882-1949) a Bulgarian Communist, head of the Bulgarian Comintern in Berlin in the late 1920s. He was arrested after the Reichstag Fire in 1933 and was accused of complicity in the plot to burn down the Reichstag. The Nazis publicly tried then subsequently acquitted him (against their will) in December of the same year following the success of his brilliant defence which André Malraux himself helped to organise. However, Dimitrov remained in custody and was eventually released from Moabit military prison in February 1934 and went on to become Prime Minister of Bulgaria.

30. **Whether it is Thälmann… or Ossietzky** *(de Thaelmann… à Ossietsky)*: In May 1933, in keeping with their policy of silencing political opposition and any anti-Nazi intellectuals who might "corrupt" through their teaching or books, the Nazis instigated public book-burning bonfires in Berlin and other German cities, as a signal that they would not tolerate any left-wing, democratic, Jewish or pacifist "anti-German" publications. As a result, many authors and intellectuals, among them Carl von Ossietzky, found themselves banned.

Chapter VIII

31. **Some Sunday worshipper's eyes** *(des yeux du dimanche)*: literally "Sunday eyes". This is surely a cross-referencing "corruption" of "les habits du dimanche" (Sunday best) and "observer le dimanche" (to keep the Sabbath holy), the inference being that, similar to a Sunday worshipper, the child should believe in the charming fairy-tale world the mother describes as she croons, seeing it through the most beautiful eyes she could possibly have given him in this earthly world.

BIOGRAPHICAL SUMMARY

[This summary confines itself to indicating the significant biographical details of Malraux's life and the dates of publication of his main literary works]

1901   Georges-André Malraux born November 3 in Paris.

1905   Parents separate. Malraux goes to live with grandmother in provinces.

1909   Grandfather killed in an accident.

1915-18 Finishes secondary education. Leaves school without obtaining the Baccalauréat.

1919   Starts work as a buyer for René-Louis Doyon, a specialist in rare books. Begins writing first articles and moves into publishing work for Kra. Publishes article, "Les origines de la poésie cubiste", in *La Connaissance*. Works for Kahnweiler.

1921   Publishes *Lunes en Papier* (Kahnweiler). Marries Clara Goldschmidt.

1922   Begins publishing regular articles for N.R.F. *(Nouvelle Revue Française)*.

1923   First archaeological expedition to Indo-China (mainly Cambodia, or "Kampuchea"). Arrested and tried in Pnom-Penh for removing bas-reliefs from one of the Buddhist temples. Sentenced to 3 years' imprisonment — this was later commuted to a 1-year suspended sentence after petitions on his behalf by many of his fellow-writers, including Aragon, Breton, Gide and Mauriac. Returns to France.

1925-26 Second visit to Indo-China. Becomes politically involved. Founds newspaper in Saigon. Publishes paper, "L'Indochine enchaînée". Becomes connected with the Kuomintang (revolutionary organisation). Returns to France.

1926   Publishes *La Tentation de l'Occident* (Grasset).

1927   Publishes "D'une jeunesse européenne" in *Écrits*, (Grasset).

1928   *Royaume Farfelu* (Gallimard). First major work *Les Conquérants*, (Grasset). Begins work at Gallimard's publishing house.

1930   *La Voie Royale* (Grasset). Malraux's father commits suicide. Malraux begins world-wide travels, including visits to India and Afghanistan.

1931   Travels in China, Japan and the U.S.

1933   Publishes *La Condition humaine* (Gallimard*)* — wins the Prix Goncourt. Birth of daughter, Florence. Own mother dies.

1934   Together with a friend, aviator Corniglion-Molinier, makes historic flight over the Yemen desert (Dhana) in search of the legendary city of the Queen of Sheba, which they claimed to have discovered.
Goes to Germany with Gide to help organise defence of Dimitrov and others in Reichstag Fire Trial. Petitions for Thälmann's and Dimitrov's release and that of other Communists.
Becomes President of the "Comité Mondial contre la guerre et le fascisme".
Goes to Moscow. Meets Trotsky, also meets Pasternak, Einstein, Gorky and Stalin. Gives speech at first "Congrès des Écrivains soviétiques" in Moscow.

1935   Publishes *Le Temps du mépris* (Gallimard).
Attends and speaks at "Congrès International des Écrivains pour la défense de la Culture" in Paris.

1936   Attends London meeting of the "Congrès International des Écrivains pour la défense de la Culture".
Outbreak of Spanish Civil War (1936-39). Goes to Spain to join International Brigade and fight for the Republicans. Creates and commands the "Escadrille España".
Separates from Clara.

1937   Attends writers' conference for "la défense de la Culture" (cf. above) in Madrid.
Fund-raiser and campaigner for the Spanish Republican Government in Europe and the U.S. Meets Hemingway, Einstein and Robert Oppenheimer.
Publishes *L'Espoir* (Gallimard).
Publishes "La Psychologie de l'Art" in *Verve*.

1938   Makes own film of *L'Espoir* in Barcelona.

1939   Outbreak of World War Two. Malraux enlists in French Army tank regiment.

1940   Captured by Germans; imprisoned. Escapes to Free Zone. Joins French Resistance movement. Becomes a *Maquis* leader.
Meetings with Sartre and other French literary figures.

1943   Publishes "La Lutte avec l'Ange" *(Les Noyers de l'Altenburg,* Éditions du Haut-Pays, Lausanne) the remaining first part of a longer novel burnt by Germans.
Continues Résistance activities.

1944   Commands an F.F.I. Brigade as "Colonel Berger". Wounded and captured. Released from prison when Nazis begin withdrawal.
Accidental death of Malraux's two brothers.

Death of mistress, Josette, mother of his two sons.
Creates and commands Alsace-Lorraine Brigade — fights in Alsace.

1945   World War Two ends. Malraux meets General De Gaulle.
Awarded the "Légion d'Honneur" (France's highest award for valour).
Becomes Minister of Information in De Gaulle's first government.

1946   Continues writing and publishing.
Resigns with De Gaulle from government.

1947   Becomes director of propaganda for the R.P.F. (Gaullist Party).
Publishes *Le Musée Imaginaire* (Skira), first major work on art history.

1948   *Les Noyers de l'Altenburg* (Gallimard).
Marries Madeleine Lioux, widow of his deceased half-brother, Roland.

1950   Begins publishing essays on art, e.g. *Saturne* (Gallimard) an essay on Goya,
and *Les Voix du Silence* (Gallimard).

1951-57 Continues activities as art historian and writer.
Maintains political connections.

1958   Publishes signed address against torture with Roger Martin du Gard, Sartre and Mauriac.
Becomes Minister of Information in De Gaulle's second government.
World-wide travels and lectures.

1959-60 Becomes Minister for Cultural Affairs.
Continues travels.

1960   Death of both of his sons in car crash.

1961   Assassination attempt (bomb) on his life by O.A.S. (Organisation in favour
of Algeria remaining under French control).
Visits U.S.A — guest of President Kennedy.

1965   Depression, illness. Travels to Far East and China. Meets Mao Tse-Tung.
Resumes writing.

1966   Renews close friendship with old friend, Louise de Vilmorin, poet and novelist.

1967-68 Publishes his *Antimémoires* (Gallimard) — an instant success.
Resumes travels and lectures. Visits London and U.S.S.R.

1969   Retires from politics. Begins permanent residence at Louise de Vilmorin's
"Verrières" home.
Death of Louise de Vilmorin. Malraux continues to live at "Verrières".

1970   Death of General De Gaulle.

1971   Resumes writing and publishing. *Les Chênes qu'on abat* (Gallimard)
        Failing health.

1972   Suffers a stroke.

1974   Publishes *Lazare* (Gallimard) and other works.
        Travels to Japan.

1975   *Hôtes de Passage* (Gallimard)

1976   *Le Miroir des Limbes* (Pléiade)
        Dies November 23 in hospital at Créteil.
        (Other works published posthumously.)

SELECT BIBLIOGRAPHY

Works by André Malraux (and editions used):

Le Temps du mépris, Gallimard, Paris, 1935.
La Condition humaine, Gallimard, Paris, 1946.
L'Espoir, Gallimard, Paris, 1960 edition.
Les Noyers de l'Altenburg, Gallimard, Paris, 1948.
Antimémoires, Gallimard, Paris, 1967.

General Studies of Malraux

Boak, D., *André Malraux*, Clarendon Press, Oxford, 1968.
Cazenave, M. (ed.), *André Malraux*, Éditions de l'Herne, Paris, 1982.
Frohock, W.M., *André Malraux and the Tragic Imagination*, Stanford University Press, Stanford, California, 1952.
Jenkins, C., *André Malraux*, Twayne Publishers Inc., New York, 1972.
Lacouture, J., *André Malraux* (Translated from the French by Alan Sheridan), André Deutsch Ltd., London, 1975.
Stéphane, R., *Fin d'une jeunesse*, Paris, 1954, p. 51.

Other General Works and bibliographical sources

Brée, G., *Camus*, Rutgers University Press, New Jersey, 1959.
Bullock, A., *Hitler: A Study in Tyranny*, Penguin, Revised edition, London, 1962.
Frei, N., *National Socialist Rule in Germany: The Führer State 1933-1945* (Translated by Simon B. Steyne), Blackwell, Oxford, 1993.
Gutman, Y. and Berenbaum, M. (eds.), *Anatomy of the Auschwitz Death Camp*, Indiana University Press, 1994 Paperback edition, 1998.
Harwood, R., *The Survival of the Self*, (Avebury Series in Philosophy), Ashgate, Aldershot, 1998.
Hebb, D.O., *A Textbook of Psychology*, W.B. Saunders Company, Philadelphia/London, 1966.
Heller, M. and Nekrich, A., *Utopia in Power: A History of the U.S.S.R. from 1917 to the Present* (Translated from the Russian by Phyllis B. Carlos), Hutchinson, London, 1986 edition.
Mann, G., *The History of Germany since 1789* (Translated from the German by Marian Jackson), Penguin Books, Peregrine edition, 1988.
Nietzsche, F., *Thus Spoke Zarathustra* (Translated by R.J. Hollingdale), Penguin Books, Middlesex, 1969 edition.
Read, A. and Fisher D., *Berlin: The Biography of a City*, Pimlico (Random House), London, 1994.
Reid, J.M.H. (ed.), *The Concise Oxford Dictionary of French Literature*, Clarendon Press, Oxford, (Paperback edition), 1976.
Todd, O., *Albert Camus: Une Vie*, Biographies N.R.F., Gallimard, Paris, 1996.

Westwood, J.N., *Endurance and Endeavour: Russian History 1812-1992*, Oxford University Press, (4th edition), 1993.

Zuckerman, M., *Psychobiology of personality*, (Series: Problems in the Behavioural Sciences), Cambridge University Press, Cambridge, 1991.

Zuckerman, Albright, Marks and Millar, *Stress and Hallucinatory Effects of Perpetual Isolation and Confinement*, Psychological Monographs: General and Applied, (Vol. 76. No. 30), No. 549, The American Psychological Association Inc., Washington, 1962.